UNDER EIGHT FLAGS

UNDER EIGHT FLAGS

3rd Book of Memoirs 1958-1991
The last 33 years at sea

Anthony F. Winstanley

Pictorial Press

Victoria, British Columbia, Canada

Copyright © 2001 Anthony F. Winstanley

Cover design : Roy Diment and Bryony Wynne-Jones

ISBN 0-9699920-2-5

Frontispiece: *M.S.T.S. General Gordon*

Published by
Pictorial Press
P.O.Box 5577, Victoria, B.C.
V8R 6S4, Canada

Printed in Canada

This book is dedicated to the memory of my mother who suggested that the sea life might suit me. To my children, who, in their early years, saw little of me because I took her advice. Despite a bad start and frequent setbacks, I eventually realized with deep gratitude that my mother's suggestion was a wise one.

By the same author

UNDER EIGHT FLAGS
Vol. I 1937-1947
The first eleven years at sea

UNDER EIGHT FLAGS
Vol. II 1948-1957
The next ten years at sea

ACKNOWLEDGEMENTS

Thanks to Captain Tom McCulloch retired Master and Captain Peter Jackson, for writing generous comments in the foreword. To Captains Hill Wilson, Roy Harrington, and Mike Carter for supplying amusing anecdotes and the kind of encouragement I looked for, and received. Thanks to Roy Diment and Malcolm MacIntosh who never failed to help when I needed it. To Frank Clapp who, once again, was generous in giving me pictures of ships that I served on. Special thanks to Peter Jones who bravely undertook the burden of publishing this book. He and his able assistant, Bryony, showed remarkable restraint when, after hours spent reading and correcting the manuscript, I wanted it back in order to add several episodes, which I wrote about in letters thirty years ago.

And finally thanks to my daughter, Bernadette, who received those letters and kept them. They contain good stories which I felt were worth re-telling.

FOREWORD

It was with the greatest pleasure that I read Tony Winstanley's first two books which described his life at sea. I was struck by the close similarity of experiences we had in common during our first years in the shipping industry. There were many reputable shipping Companies prior to the Second World War who operated their own training schemes for teenagers who wished to take up a seagoing career as deck officers. They taught navigation, seamanship and general ship management, along with safe practices and the carriage of cargo. Such companies were difficult to get into, mainly because they had such a wide choice. Such an apprenticeship required dedication; it involved long hours, hard work, sometimes poor conditions and many months, sometimes years away from home. After apprenticeship there were three monumentally difficult examinations to be passed before finally becoming a Master Mariner. The task was daunting.

My own time at sea during the Second World War included being torpedoed and spending time in an open lifeboat. After the War, Tony's and my paths diverged. For my part, I joined Cunard White Star, as it was then known, and stayed with that Company until I retired, thirty-seven years later. Eventually, having served in all the great passenger ships of that Company, I commanded "QE2" for a total of seven years, and had the honour of taking her to the South Atlantic at the time of the Falklands crisis.

Recently I had the privilege of meeting Tony Winstanley and we spent several hours together reminiscing about the days which involved our common interest. Times have changed and technology has moved on to radically alter the way ships now operate, but it was good to speak about those days which we both knew so well.

Peter Jackson
Master.(Retired)
"Queen Elizabeth 2"

FOREWORD (Additional)

Tony Winstanley's 3rd volume of "Under Eight Flags" starts with his return to Canada in 1958 and ends in 1991 with his final voyage on the BC coast. In between these dates the pages are full of interesting information about his seafaring career around the globe and aboard an amazing variety of vessels. He is a bit of a rebel about some of the appalling situations in which he found himself, but through it all his abiding love of the sea and ships shines through.

His description of the weather at station Poppa in the Pacific Ocean is a classic. One feels one is aboard the *Whitethroat* lying helpless in the trough between gigantic waves that towered over her very existence.

From H.M.C. Dockyard, Tony moved on to the Vietnam war, sailing in ships of the U.S. Military Sea Transportation Service. His account of the difference between local seagoing practices and the American counterpart is fascinating and informative. Obviously he enjoyed his sojourn with the Yankees while taking due note of their foibles. His description of troopship voyages to various ports in Vietnam, is well done. The tension in the war zone is all too clear, and the involvement of South Korean troops in Vietnam is an item of information I had forgotten about. A real Winstanley episode is the time he was hospitalized in Pusan and Seoul with villains and heroines in good supply, and with virtue triumphant in the end.

Back in Canada he returns to West Coast vessels and there is lots of interaction with miserable skippers and recalcitrant crew members. Although not a big man, he never seems to have backed away from confrontation or threat of violence. A more enjoyable period of his life followed when he signed on with B.C. Ferries after a short interlude in the West Indies on the bauxite trade. When he returned to Canada, it was, in his own words, "To the perfect job, ten days on, five days off, and every night at home." Life was not dull as Tony illustrates, when he describes his early attempts at achieving a smooth docking and proper stowage of automobiles.

His retirement from B.C. ferries did not see him inactive for long, but he finally decided to call it quits at age seventy-one. This was following a miserable voyage on a ship chartered to do forestry research on the B.C. coast. A truly remarkable saga of determination and nautical professionalism covering many years, was at an end.

I first met the author in April 1941 when we were both serving as cadets on the *Mandalay*; a Paddy Henderson ship discharging cargo in South Sandon Dock, Liverpool. He had completed his four years cadetship and was about to go ashore for his 2nd mate's certificate. Probably his unusual name and his confident appearance all combined to lock him in some part of my brain. Many years later my attention was drawn to a brief comment in a seafaring publication that recommended readers to a book called "Under Eight Flags", written by a fellow called Winstanley who lived only a short distance away in Victoria. Could this be the same man? It was! And we have been close friends ever since.

T. D. McCulloch.
Master Mariner. F.G.

CONTENTS

AUTHOR'S PREFACE

Over the past few months, several people have enquired when the final volume of "Under Eight Flags" would be finished. I felt flattered that they should be interested enough to ask. As for myself I wondered whether it would ever be completed. After three years of blood, sweat, and sometimes tears, it is finally going to press. Some of the events were easy to write about, and those were during the happy days ashore and afloat. It was more difficult to remember the hard times, and I had doubts about even recording some of them, for fear of possibly offending people. I confided in a good friend and asked his opinion. He thought that in order to write a truthful account of events as I saw them, it should not be a watered down version. "Tell it as it happened" he said. Good advice. So I have tried to do exactly that, but hasten to add that in so doing, I do not wish to offend anyone.

I wish to thank my family and friends who have so generously assisted me in writing this book, particularly when I had problems with my computer. Thanks to my son Martin who gave me the wretched machine in the first place. I admit that it has been useful, although there have been times when I felt like throwing a brick at it, particularly when it read, " There is a serious defect with the floppy disc. Do you wish to continue?" What a silly question, of course I did. But I needed help. That came in the person of my daughter Veronica, who never complained about my continual pleas for assistance.

1

Return to Canada

It was on a windy, wet evening in November 1958 when Celia and I, with our seven children, walked up the gangway of the splendid, Canadian Pacific liner, *Empress of England*. The 26,000 ton ship lay alongside the Princes Pier, Liverpool, and was about to sail for Montreal. I was anxious to return to Canada to make a fresh start. Things would be different this time; no more long sea voyages. I would find a steady job on coastal ships.

Conditions aboard the *Empress of England* were far better than those we had endured ten years earlier aboard the United States Lines *Marine Tiger*. We were now accommodated in two comfortable cabins in the fore-end of the ship, immediately above the ship's port stabilizer machinery. This was soon to be in operation, once the ship cleared the top of Ireland and entered the Atlantic Ocean.

I knew enough about the passage across the Western Ocean in winter time to expect that we would get a good dusting and I wasn't disappointed. The hum from the stabilizer machinery increased to a whine as the fins, which projected from the hull, fought to dampen the ship's roll. This was achieved with some success but the heave and pitch of the ship was not affected and a day after leaving Liverpool we were battling into the teeth of a full westerly gale. The ship's bows descended into a sickening abyss, there was a heavy thump and hundreds of tons of the cold Atlantic crashed onto the fo'c's'le head.

Before the onslaught the children had discovered that there was plenty of good food aboard, now some of them were about to dispose of it. I wasn't feeling so good myself, but it was of vital importance to my standing as head of the family not to reveal this apparent weakness. Fortunately I was able to do this by putting on a demonstration of how seamen countered the movement of the ship by swaying in the opposite direction and treating the ship's tantrums as a huge joke. The children didn't think it was funny and when Andrew's complexion

13

took on a greenish hue during supper in the tourist dining room, I hustled him towards the elevator. He needed the fresh air of the open deck, but before we arrived there he deposited his supper on the elevator floor! My sympathies were divided equally between Andrew and the uncomplaining steward who arrived to clean it up.

Our train trip across Canada from Montreal to Vancouver was less of an ordeal than the previous one in 1948. Trans-Canadian rail travel had improved a bit, food was less expensive, the rolling stock was of post-war vintage and our porter helpful. Still, after days of tedium spent looking out across the endless plains, it was a relief to be among the Rocky mountains. A day later we lumbered into rain soaked Vancouver. We were home again.

2

The *Canora*

Shortly after we had settled in our house at Deep Cove I found a 3rd mate's job with the Canadian National Steamships. It wasn't the sort of job I wanted as I did not enjoy working for this stingy company, but the need was urgent. Our money had run out.

The *Canora* was a strange looking vessel of about 3000 tons with twin funnels abreast of each other. She was powered by a steam reciprocating engine which turned a shaft that ran the length of the vessel with a propeller at both ends. When under way both screws turned simultaneously so that the one in the bow had a pulling effect. Viewed from a distance at sea it was difficult to distinguish bow from stern, and as she was capable of little more than eight knots she often appeared to be stationary. She was built in 1919 in Eastern Canada and designed to carry passenger rail cars from the mainland to Victoria. This service had long since been discontinued and now she carried railway boxcars to various ports on Vancouver Island.

In order to join the *Canora* I had to lug my bags aboard a series of buses to reach a point twenty miles east of Vancouver where a taxi took me along a dusty track that followed the bank of the mighty Fraser River. The ship appeared in the distance as if she was lying in the midst of a clump of scrub bushes, box cars and repair shops. We were miles from habitation of any kind. This god-forsaken spot was known as Port Mann, the main marshalling yard for hundreds of rail cars owned by the Canadian National Railways.

The ship's master was an irascible Scot named Patterson who was standing on the bridge when I stepped off the gangway. With an imperious wave of his hand, he gruffly ordered me to bring my seaman's discharge book into his room to sign the ship's articles. Captain Patterson had once served aboard deep sea ships and wanted to run the *Canora* as if she was an ocean going vessel. There was to be no easy going familiarity between him and the crew and that included

15

the officers. They could address each other by their first names but nobody called the *old man* Donald. To some he was known as "Musheater."

The *Canora* was not a happy ship. Part of the reason was money, or lack of it. The Canadian National Steamship Company was not generous in rewarding employees for their efforts. The accommodation was poor, particularly for the seamen and engine crew. A dozen men housed in one deck house was considered adequate, yet the disused passenger rooms could have been converted for the use of the crew. Nobody seems to have thought of that.

I had only been aboard a few days when I found myself in trouble with the *old man*. When using the officer's toilet I had noticed a piece of paper attached to the door, which seemed to indicate a schedule of cleaning to be kept by the officers. It was signed by the master, and also signed by the last officer who had supposedly done the job. I read this notice several times in order to convince myself that it was real, not a mischievous joke on a new officer. I asked the 2nd mate what he thought about the funny notice. "It's no joke, and it's your turn today." Jack Robinson was a serious fellow in his late thirties, who had a master's ticket and his aim was to get enough experience on the Fraser River to qualify for a pilots job. He was anxious not to jeopardize his chances by making a fuss about cleaning toilets. I took a different view saying that I hadn't signed on as a ship's officer to clean toilets. "In that case, don't bother me, you should speak to the *old man*." It wasn't the kind of reaction I had expected from a fellow officer, and it only stiffened my resolve not to "toe the line" regarding cleaning duties.

News of my insubordination reached the *old man* sooner than expected and he called me to his room. Captain Patterson was not accustomed to seeing his orders ignored. He was a big man who adopted a forceful manner when faced with disobedience. He stood up from his desk, folded his arms on his chest, stuck out his chin and said, "Mr. Winstanley, I understand that it is your turn to clean the officer's toilet today. Refusal to obey an order aboard ship can have serious consequences."

I remembered the row I had caused on the *Mandalay* in 1941 when refusing to obey the mate's order to clean up food which had been spilled into a lifeboat. But this was different. It was peacetime, besides there was a principle at stake. Taking the bull by the horns, I

16

said, "I did not sign-on as 3rd mate to clean toilets." Captain Patterson's complexion took on a different hue as his blood pressure rose. There was an ominous pause as he struggled to control his anger. All this fuss over a toilet, I thought as I waited for the control gates to burst. "You refuse to obey my orders then?" Perhaps my job was on the line, and I had only just started. How could I justify this when work was hard to find? But there was no going back now. "I will not clean toilets and that's final" I muttered, feeling a muted sense of the justness of my stand. I was tempted to add that I did not take in washing either, but thought better of it. The old man was in no mood for such jocular banter.

It did occur to me that my removal was now imminent but to my surprise he merely said, "You haven't heard the last of this, I will take it to the head office in Vancouver." In due course my name was removed from the cleaning schedule, and not surprisingly I never heard the subject mentioned again. The absurdity of the whole thing must have dawned on the old man and to give him his due, the notice disappeared from the toilet and the matter was forgotten.

It was mid winter when I joined the Canora and I became aware that conditions aboard were little better than on a pre- war deep-sea tramp. We had arrived in Victoria in the evening of a cold winter's day. The rail cars had been unloaded and as we would not sail back to the mainland until the next day, the ship was shut down for the night. As she lay some distance from the city there was little reason to go ashore. After a long day on the bridge I was relaxing in my cabin reading a book when the quartermaster came to the door, carrying a can of oil. Earlier I had seen him enter the mate's room "What the hell is that for." I asked. There was a strained silence and no reply was forthcoming until the mate appeared in the alleyway having heard my query. "You have only just come aboard and are complaining already" he said irritably. "You are godammed lucky to have a job. The power will be off in a few minutes, and you better make the best of it." Mr. Sommerville, a humourless man in his dotage was on the verge of retirement and not about to create a fuss about anything. He had been with the company so long his whole existence revolved around the Canadian National. He knew no other life and as far as he was concerned they knew what was best for the crew.

I had noticed an ancient brass oil lamp slung in gimbals on the bulkhead in my cabin. It was the same sort of lamp we had aboard the tramps in pre-war days. An odd decoration, I thought, not attaching any importance to such bric-a-brac. With memories of life aboard British tramps still fresh in my mind, I couldn't resist taunting the mate. "Do you mean to tell me that in this year of 1958 the government of a rich country like Canada is so hard-up, that they cannot connect us to shore power overnight? What about heat, will the chief engineer shut the steam off too?" The mate wrung his hands in annoyance, "Why are you grumbling to me about it for Christ's sake, the power is always turned off when we are in Victoria. What's wrong with an oil lamp anyway?" Any further argument was fruitless. I slunk into my room, lit the oil lamp as I had done many times aboard the Old man*dalay* while in Glasgow twenty years earlier, found a book, a blanket and settled down for a quiet night. The rattle of a generator ceased, the electric light faded, and we were back in the Dark Ages. The only sound was cursing from someone down the alleyway who hadn't lit his oil lamp. .

But life aboard the *Canora* wasn't all bad. I had made a few friends. One was the 3rd Engineer John Henderson. He had been in the Canadian Navy and deep-sea merchant ships, so we could talk for hours about ships, seamen and adventures in foreign ports; subjects which were never exhausted. I owe him a considerable debt, not only for helping to make life aboard more tolerable, but because he owned a car and I didn't. This meant that he was generous enough to give me a lift to Deep Cove and back to the ship at the end of shore leave.

Morale aboard did improve when "Musheater" went ashore on leave. His replacement was Captain Pugh, a tall, quiet, balding man in his sixties with a pallid complexion. He did not look at all well and seldom spoke to anyone except "Musheater" who bullied him. Because every time the ship returned to Port Mann, Captain Pugh was called to the phone on the dock to inform Captain Patterson of the days events! Even on leave ashore Captain Patterson's thoughts were on the ship. He acted as if he owned the *Canora*. It seems that he was loathe to leave her and could hardly bear the thought that another man could look after the ship properly in his absence.

Within minutes of my arrival, a loud rumbling came from below the decks and the *Canora* began to take a list. We were loading a string of box cars filled with grain, each weighing 60 tons or more. I had seen a similar operation a year earlier on Lake Okanagan, but on the *Canora* the crew did not have to load or discharge the cargo. This was done by rail workers.

It was now the freshet season on the river. Warm spring weather was melting the snow in the mountains of the Coast Range and turning a normally placid river into a raging torrent. It threatened to spill over its banks before dispersing out into the salty waters of the Gulf of Georgia. When running down river with an ebb tide, plus the freshet, the *Canora* would achieve remarkable speeds. Navigating was a tricky business and required the knowledge and skill of the master. It was made more hazardous by the presence of a fleet of fish boats choking the fairway from bank to bank. The fishermen were gill-netters whose nets were supported by a line of wooden floats strung out over the stern for a distance of several hundred feet. The end of each net was marked by a flag.

The fishermen were obliged to keep the channel clear for on-coming traffic. It was in their best interests to avoid having their nets cut but it was often a nail-biting time for men in the wheelhouses of deep-sea ships, tugs, and coastal vessels like the *Canora*. These vessels would sound blasts on their steam whistles and air horns but sometimes this failed to stir the errant fishermen who would wait until the last minute before hauling in their nets. The air above the Fraser was blue with obscenities.

The arrival of a railcar loaded with scrap, bound for Japan, was always welcomed by the crew of the *Canora*. They could then augment their meagre wages by helping themselves to the contents during the trip across to Victoria. Under cover of darkness it was a simple matter to climb into the pile of scrap metal and remove pieces of copper and brass. These were hidden from view until the opportunity came to carry them ashore to the closest scrap dealer willing to pay cash, and no questions asked.

The cooks on the *Canora* had their own business sideline which involved the ship's stores. As the food was good and in plentiful supply there was no reason to complain, but there was evidently a surplus aboard and this had to be disposed of. After we had worked for a month a relief crew came aboard. They were a welcome sight, but the change of crew had to be done quickly in order not to delay the ship, so there was little time to exchange pleasantries. I was leaning over the rail watching two cooks struggling down the gangway with their heavy bags. They were met by a pack of hungry, stray dogs which sniffed at one bag from which blood was dripping. "Get off, get the hell away you filthy hounds" shouted the cook, anxious to gain the safety of his car a hundred yards away. "Look at those thieving bastards" said John, who had appeared on deck and was about to accompany me ashore. "There are a couple of roasts and a ham or two which the crew won't be getting. No wonder the company doesn't want to pay us a decent wage!"

Larceny of another kind was practiced ashore and this time the crew were the victims. Their cars lay idle for a month while their owners worked aboard the ship. They were parked in waste land of thick scrub grass near the railroad tracks. A rough road led from there to the main road. On one occasion four tired men from the engine staff trudged ashore in the fading light anxious to go home on leave. They got into a car, the motor was started, the clutch engaged, but to the consternation of the driver there was a whirring sound but the car did not move an inch. After the passengers had expressed their opinions of the car, the disgusted owner, holding a flashlight, got out to inspect his vehicle. It wasn't until he directed the light under the rear of the car that he discovered the entire rear wheel assembly was missing!

After a few months aboard the *Canora*, I began to become increasingly anxious about my future. Rumours had begun to circulate that the company was about to lay -up ships and lay off personnel. Although I did not enjoy my job the prospect of having to search for another was not a happy one. But the pall of gloom which had descended on the family was immediately lifted, when I heard that a 3rd mates job was available. It was with the Canadian Naval Auxiliary Fleet based at Esquimalt in Victoria, the Provincial capital on Vancouver Island.

While on my days off from the *Canora*, I crossed over to the island and secured an interview with the Marine Superintendent. To my astonishment and relief, I was given a friendly reception and told I would be required immediately. When I explained that my family lived on the mainland, and I needed time to dispose of our house and find somewhere to live in Victoria, he was sympathetic. " Settle your affairs, and call me when you can start work." This was a change from the usual attitude of employers. Things were looking up.

3

Her Majesty's Dockyard

To hurriedly pull up stakes after ten years was no easy matter. There were a thousand things to attend to and little time and money to accomplish it. However, spurred on by the prospect of new surroundings, a better job and future, we began to pack-up our belongings. A real estate agent was hired and he assured us that he had our best interests at heart. We thought that our property was worth $4500 but unknown to us the real estate agent was disdainful, pointing out to prospective buyers all the things that were wrong with it, saying that it was only worth $3500. People were brought along to view it. We found it a humiliating experience as couples shuffled from one room to another in a critical way. A fussy woman expressed her disapproval of the small bedrooms and lack of plugs for all her electrical appliances, while her husband wanted to know where he could put his collection of tools; I was tempted to tell him but was afraid to lose a buyer. They wanted a house with a basement, a fireplace and more than one toilet. Our house lacked all these refinements.

I became aware that in spite of my strenuous efforts to improve its livability, "Journeys' End" had serious shortcomings. On the other hand, for a man with the means and ability to fix it up, it was a bargain. There was a demand for properties such as ours, why then, were there no buyers? We learned the answer to that question when a friend, Cyril Monk, posing as a client was taken aside by the wily real estate agent who pointed out all the things that were wrong with "Journey's End." He had evidently dissuaded other customers from buying the property! Cyril, being a crafty fellow, knew a thing or two about real estate having made some judicious land purchases himself. He suspected that the agent was after the property himself. The agent knew that I was desperate to get rid of it and he would do us a "favour" by "taking it off our hands," then sell it at a handsome profit when the right customer came along. Cyril beat him to it. He offered us exactly what we were asking and we were relieved to be rid of it.

At first, my job in the Canadian Naval Auxiliaries seemed ideal. It offered steady employment, prospects of promotion, short sea voyages and life in the pleasant city of Victoria. What I didn't know was that there was a price to pay for what appeared to be the perfect job. As anyone who has worked for the Federal Government knows, the pay was abysmally poor and there were frustrations about working in the dockyard which produced a kind of torpor, a state of mind akin to being in a trance. I had discovered a place where it was not only possible but easy to hold onto a job without the need to exert myself.

When walking through the Dockyard Gates at Esquimalt one entered a place in the grip of chronic inertia and ennui. The grey painted ships of the auxiliary fleet, lay at their berths among the frigates and destroyers of the navy. Some of the ships ventured out of the harbour when required, others lay stationary for weeks on end. The purpose of auxiliary ships was to provide oil and supplies to the naval ships, to tow targets for gunnery practice, dump old ammunition, and other sundry duties required in running a navy.

The tugs *Clifton* and *Heatherington* towed targets out into the Straits and the naval ships took pot shots at them until it was time to return to the dock for supper and shore leave. The *Oshawa*, an ex-minesweeper, and the *Whitethroat*, a North Sea trawler were used for ocean research work. The *Dundurn*, a small tanker, made a trip across the harbour about twice a week to load bunkers for the fleet, thus amassing a monthly run of 10 nautical miles and consuming a total of 50 gallons of diesel fuel. Her crew didn't get much sea time in as she seldom went out of the harbour.

The two crews of the fire tug accrued even less sea time, and a job in this vessel was considered as semi-retirement. These crews worked twelve hour watches. The day watch polishing the brass and washing the deck, took things easy as there was little else to do until the arrival of their reliefs at 6pm. Once a week the engine was started, the lines let go, and the tug taken out into the harbour to test the equipment. After squirting streams of water across the harbour the crew packed up for the day and returned to rest alongside the dock.

The night watch came on duty at 6pm. After having a leisurely supper they could then play cards, or read stimulating literature before taking to their bunks for the night. The fireboat skippers had the softest job in the dockyard; it was a lifetime sinecure and only retirement or premature death left a vacancy. In fact it was rumoured that one night in the fire shack (a small building on the dock to house the expectant fire tug crew) the boys were in the middle of a poker game when someone remarked that he did not like the unpleasant odour, and where was Del the fireman? He hadn't been seen for two days. "That's him fast asleep in his bunk" said the engineer with a chuckle, "he likes his kip, I've seen him saw logs for twelve hours straight." "Well its time to get him on his feet, we will be knocking off soon" said the skipper with some authority. He went across the room to rouse the recumbent Del, who couldn't be woken because he was dead! Not from over exertion but quite likely from sheer boredom. By no stretch of the imagination could service aboard the fire tug be described as anything but tranquil. Fortunately for the crew, dockyard fires were rare so the opportunities for the crew to prove themselves were almost non existent.

In peacetime the whole operation in the yard was a rather leisurely affair; there was no urgency, and therefore no need to hurry. Naval Dockyards throughout the world were, it seems, run in a similar manner. Some ships never moved for weeks on end, others were in a perpetual state of refit because the Government had allotted a few million dollars for upkeep and it had to be spent. When a vessel was declared redundant and destined for the scrap-yard, she was given an expensive refit before the ensign was lowered for the last time. Sometimes the government sold them to a third world navy which would run them for another thirty years.

It may seem an unfair comment on the rest of the Dockyard activities, but as far as the Auxiliary vessels were concerned it is fitting. However all the ships were not idle. The *Whitethroat* and *Oshawa* would put to sea for six or seven weeks doing research work for the Pacific Naval Laboratory. These were the ships in which I was destined to spend most of my time.

There were two kinds of employees in the fleet. Those who like myself, were anxious to make as much money as possible in order to support a family, and who went to sea in order to avail ourselves of the little extra cash. The others, mostly amateur seamen, who apparently did not require a decent wage and had little desire to go to sea if it could be avoided. They enjoyed a source of income elsewhere, or had wives who provided it, and for them their job in the yard was a soft berth ashore. A sinecure, merely a hobby to be carefully nurtured until retirement. These were the men in the Maintenance Department. They were responsible for fixing ship's equipment, and were available for sea duty when required. Some were allergic to shipboard life and always had a good excuse for not going to sea.

The main activity in the Maintenance Department seems to have been the making and accumulation of articles known as "rabbits." A "rabbit" was anything owned by the government which could be smuggled through the dockyard gates and used elsewhere. Several maintenance men were avid gun fanciers and the manufacture of gun stocks became one of the main items for "export." Other men used their considerable talents to construct "rabbits" for use at home, and it was the boast of one man that he had equipped the basement of his house with booty filched from H.M.C. Dockyard and it was common knowledge that some houses in Victoria were painted battleship grey.

A naval commander was reputed to have taken this activity very seriously. His rank enabled him to take his car into the Dockyard and, as he was in charge of the construction of ship components, he could park it close to the machine shop. Some clever work had been done to reinforce the underside of his car which enabled the commander to spirit away lengths of steel piping, required for plumbing jobs at home. The heavily laden car would stagger out through the Dockyard gate right under the nose of the commissionaire who being an ex-naval man himself, signaled his approval with a salute.

Another enterprising "rabbiteer" wore a large overcoat when going home after his shift in the machine shop. Secret pockets had been sewn into the lining and these were strong enough to hold weighty pieces of hardware. He had made many successful runs out of the gate until the day when he approached the gate just as the bus was about to leave. He immediately broke into a trot in a desperate effort to catch it, but heavily laden, his pockets bulging with ill-gotten gains, this last minute spurt carried away the seams. Ball bearings, couplings and assorted fittings dropped from his coat and rolled along the road in full view of startled onlookers. Whether he lost his job was not recorded. He certainly lost his bearings!

It was odd how ship's equipment was apt to disappear ashore at a time when it was most needed aboard. A case in point concerned one auxiliary ship which left the dock one morning to conduct trials off the coast. It was customary for the master when manoeuvering in the harbour, to order the helmsman to put the ship's head on a certain point ashore, until the ship was out in open waters, where a compass course was steered. This was done and the ship was finally steaming past Fisgard Pt., clear of Esquimalt harbour, when she entered a patch of thick fog. The master gave the order to steer a compass course. The helmsman peered into the binnacle but was unable to see anything. The binnacle cap was hurriedly removed and to the amazement of all, the compass was missing! The ship was turned about by an angry master who felt his way carefully back into the harbour, no doubt on the war path to find who was responsible for lifting the wheelhouse compass. It transpired that a work order for the compass to be serviced had been received by the instrument shop and without telling anyone of his intentions, a technician had walked aboard, removed the compass, and taken it ashore.

4

The *Laymore*

My first ship was the *Laymore* a twin screw, 11 knot cargo vessel of about 800 displacement tons, 175 feet long, driven by high speed GM diesels. She was built in the States during the war for the transport of supplies for the army. The Canadian Navy acquired her in 1951. When I joined her she had just ceased making voyages to Monterey, California to bring sand to the dockyard for sandblasting ship's hulls. This operation ended when it was discovered that there was an abundance of sand with a high silicone content on Vancouver Island. This came as a relief to the crew because these trips were often very uncomfortable, particularly on the return trip when heavily loaded, she pounded and slammed into rough head seas almost to the point of destruction. I saw her later in dry-dock and her forward hull plating looked like corrugated steel roofing.

At first my job as 3rd mate on the *Laymore* was easy enough, as it became apparent that she spent most of the time alongside the dock. What little work went on was "routine maintenance", which for the officers, meant appearing on board each day to supervise the crew. Of course the ship looked immaculately clean, the slightest sign of rust activated a detail of men to remove it from sight with a coat of paint.

Not having a car, I went to work by bus which put me off near the dockyard gate. From there I walked past the red bricked offices and repair shops to the wharf. At first I was anxious to arrive on time having just left the world of commercial shipping where tardiness in starting work was a sin. But in the Dockyard there was no need to hurry, the ship wasn't sailing and the crew would eventually turn up. The *Laymore* carried a crew of 20 men, which was about twice as many required to run her in commercial use.

The master was a slightly built, bespectacled French Canadian, who had distinguished himself during the war as a commander of a frigate. He arrived aboard at 10 a.m. (coffee time), when the mates and engineers had gathered in the wardroom to hear what, if anything he had to say. As 3rd mate my duties were to look after stores; this included counting items of ship's bedding to be sent to the laundry and there was a knack in stretching out this work to ensure that it lasted well into the afternoon. After the sheets were bundled-up, a truck was ordered to take them to the laundry. The two seamen working with me "knew the ropes," and told me that the custom was not to order the truck before 1300 hr's, otherwise it would cut into lunch hour (which usually lasted two hours) and that was unwise. The afternoon siesta evidently was one of the perks of a job in the dockyard, and any activity which impinged on rest time was just not done.

The most important book aboard the ship was the stores book. This book was at least ten pounds in weight and over a thousand pages long. It listed in detail every nut, screw, bolt, lever, pipe and flange plus a million other items required to run a navy; everything from paper clips to mooring ropes. A great deal of time was spent by engineers and mates trying to decipher this manual, the varied sizes, shapes and types of material was mind boggling. Each item in the catalogue had a NATO number which was ten digits long, thus if a wrong number was inserted on the order sheet it might result in delivery (weeks later) of a large socket wrench instead of a pair of dividers.

I heard of a slip-up when the steward of one ship ordered salt for table use. The wrong NATO number was sent and a hundred 50 lb. sacks of road salt were delivered to the ship. I recall the occasion aboard another ship when I received word that a roll of sounding paper, (ordered weeks before) had arrived at the stores depot in Colwood. This item weighing less than two pounds could not be sent to the ship, it had to be collected and signed for. The procedure was to order transport which I did at 10 am. To my surprise a 3 ton truck arrived at noon, the driver, an ex navy lad, was delighted to have something to do, and better still a chance to stop for lunch at the Half Way House pub on the way back. The six mile round trip had cut into his lunch hour and by the time I returned aboard with the roll of sounding paper, it was time to knock-off.

After nap-time, return to work was desultory and the crew began to show signs of restlessness. Whatever work was in progress, it began to wind-down at 4pm. Paint brushes were cleaned, mops and brushes put away in preparation for a quick dash down the gangway. It was important to observe when the master went ashore. When he did, he was usually accompanied by the chief engineer and this was the signal that the rest of the crew could now take-off. This they did after a decent pause to allow the master to disappear behind the dockside buildings. The timing of this exodus largely depended on the ship's location. If she was unfortunate enough to be alongside the berth directly in view of the harbourmaster's office, she came under the close scrutiny of superintendents who monitored such activities. Masters were reminded that their crews were paid for working an eight hour day and premature knocking off would not be tolerated.

Masters and chief engineers were allowed to drive their cars into the dockyard and park near the ship. Lesser ranks had to walk half a mile to a parking lot up a hill on the road to Victoria and this was not far from the closest "watering hole" to the Dockyard. The Tudor House was well-patronised. Those with money to spend could take a breather and discuss the days events with their shipmates before heading home.

Misunderstandings sometimes occurred because of differences in nautical parlance used by naval and merchant service personnel. One day I was standing on the foc'sle head of the *Laymore* as we entered the old drydock in Esquimalt. A bow line was sent ashore, the eye put on to a bollard and we took up the slack. As we moved into position the dockmaster gave orders through his megaphone. "Down slack, mate." I complied by telling the bosun to slack away the line. No sooner had he done so when the dockmaster bellowed up at us, " I told you to down slack, and I mean down slack." Stung by what I considered as an insulting criticism of our efficiency, I shouted back, "What the hell do you think we are doing, the line is slack." Matters would have deteriorated further had not one one of our seaman hastened to tell me that the order "Down slack" in naval terms, meant take up the slack. How very odd, the exact opposite of what it meant to a merchant seaman.

5

Dumping Ammo

About twice a month the *Laymore* made a run to Vancouver to pick-up stores. It was about a six hour run and considered a pleasure trip for those with enough money to spend a night ashore. But trips to the west coast to dump ammunition were far from fun, as the *Laymore* was a lively vessel in a rough sea.

When the cruiser *Ontario* was scrapped, there was no further use for her 6 inch shells; several hundred rounds had to be disposedof. They were dumped into the sea about 30 miles off the West Coast, in an area shown by a dotted line on the chart as "Caution, Explosives Dumping Area." We loaded about 300 tons of ammunition at Rocky Point and headed out along the Straits of Juan de Fuca and out into the open Pacific.

There was usually a swell at the entrance to the Juan de Fuca Straits and sometimes sea conditions made the operation difficult. In order to reduce rolling, when dumping was in progress, the engines were run at slow speed and a course steered to achieve this. The winchman who worked both winches, had to be skilled enough to prevent the pallet board, on which two shells were strapped, from swinging about wildly as it was lifted out of the hold and over the side. The hatch tender held a trip line which he pulled at the right moment to release the load into the sea.

On one trip we experienced rougher weather than usual. I was on watch when we reached the dumping area before midnight. The engines were reduced to slow ahead, deck lights were switched on, seamen came on deck, trimmed the derricks and opened the hatch. But there was a heavy swell and no matter which course we steered the pitching and rolling was so violent that the *old man* considered it too dangerous to unload the cargo. The men working on deck could hardly keep their footing. He considered abandoning the operation and seeking shelter until the weather moderated, but, anxious to get the job finished, he changed his mind and ordered work to begin. I stood on the wing of the bridge bracing myself against a stanchion in order to remain upright.

Before long a heavy sea broke over the starboard side. Someone shouted, "Look out on deck!" The sea lifted a 15 foot boat, which lay athwartships at the end of the hatch, and carried it overboard on the port side. The following sea was even heavier and the next roll to port lifted the boat back aboard! The *old man* had had enough. We increased speed, altered course, the boat was secured, the hatch covered and we waited for sea conditions to moderate. It was a great relief when a few hours later the last load went over the side, the hatch was battened down, the engines put full ahead, and we headed for the Straits of Juan de Fuca, and home.

6

A home under constant repair

For all the early frustration I felt about my job in the Dockyard there was one compensation; I now spent more time ashore than I had ever done since first going to sea. Soon after our arrival in Victoria we moved into a large old house which we rented for more than we could afford. We needed time to find a house of our own. Then I made the mistake of buying a car with money which should have been saved for a down payment on a house. I was tired of buying other people's cast-offs, this time I would own a more up to date model. I bought a 1951 Chrysler, a car large enough to contain all of us in comfort. It had a quite luxurious interior with spotless, blue upholstery and an imposing array of buttons and switches. It also had an automatic transmission. Very grand indeed. However as soon as I drove it away from the dealer I had the feeling that it was far too posh a car for anyone with my income. A doctor or lawyer's vehicle perhaps, but not for the 3rd mate of the *Laymore*, it just didn't fit. I had a premonition that I would not own it for long, and for once I was right.

It soon became clear that our living expenses, plus the running costs of the grand Chrysler, were more than my meagre wages could sustain. Our savings were being depleted at an alarming rate and there would be nothing left for a down payment on a house. As it happened we looked at a dilapidated old house which the wily real estate agent said was a "Real bargain", but in the same breath he regretted to have to tell us that we could not meet the down payment. We may have appeared crestfallen until he said, "But wait, I think we can make a deal!" He had his eye on my car. "What is it worth"? he asked, rubbing his hands together. Being honest and naive, I replied that I had paid a $1100 for it. His face lit up. " I will tell you what I can do, its a great deal for you, we can exchange cars and the house is yours." This seemed like a generous offer. More to the point, it relieved me of the guilt I had felt about owning a car which was beyond our means.

To this day I am not sure who got the better deal. I do know that we owned a run-down, uncomfortable house and an even more decrepit car. It too was a Chrysler, fifteen years old and showing signs of abuse. The car caused us no end of trouble during the next few months. I was never sure whether it would start when it was time to go to work, and if it did, whether it would take me there. The engine finally expired and the wretched machine was taken away for scrap. I returned to bus travel and found it less nerve wracking.

Our house was on a quiet street which was near the line dividing the exclusive residential area of Oak Bay and the City of Victoria. To those who aspired to climb the social ladder, a house in the former was considered a good start. We lived on the other side of the "Great Divide." The house at 1052 Amphion Street (named after H.M.S. Amphion, a warship that docked in Esquimalt a century ago) was built in the early years of this century. I judged this to be about 1903 because of newspapers of that date, which I found in the space between the roof and ceiling. They were stuffed between the joists as a crude form of insulation. The house was a two-storey, wooden structure. The outside walls were covered with cedar shingles, as was the roof and a crude addition had been built later. It contained the kitchen which looked out to a seldom used verandah. This verandah had a permanent slope to it, because the blocks supporting at one end had rotted.

The house lacked several important essentials; the heating was totally inadequate. There was a wood stove in the kitchen which was supposed to provide heat in a two-storied house with no insulation. This meant that the house was damp during the winter months causing a coating of mildew to cover the walls in some rooms. There was no basement, and very little cupboard space. There was also only one toilet, which was in the same room as the bathroom. With a big family this last item was to prove a distinct disadvantage.

Whoever built the house must have put it up in his spare time. Possibly he wasn't feeling well, didn't possess a spirit level, or had a severe case of vertigo because nothing in its construction seemed to fit properly. I discovered this when I tried to put up wallpaper in a bedroom. As the ceilings were ten feet high this was no easy task. In the days before wallpaper was pre-glued, it had to be laid flat and pasted. Being the cheapest I could find, it was little more than tissue and would tear if breathed on heavily. After I had put up six or seven sheets, (a very tricky operation particularly if the pattern had to be matched), I found to my intense anger that the end piece was at least two inches away from where the ceiling and wall met. In other words, the room was "out of whack," not square. When the job was finished the result was hardly edifying for long creases ran along places where I had been unable to iron them out. In most places the pattern on one strip of paper didn't match the pattern on the next piece. But at this point my patience ran out. I was beyond caring and went in search of a hammer to take my frustration out on a piece of wallboard which had become detached.

After the water had backed-up into the kitchen sink, I removed a few shingles from the side of the house and crawled under it to investigate the cause. It was a tight squeeze as the clearance between the floor and the ground was no more than a foot. The air was damp and fetid. In all likelihood this space had been undisturbed for more than half a century. Holding a flashlight, I crawled and clawed myself along at a snails pace through curtains of cobwebs, over the skeleton of a cat and miscellaneous rubbish, towards the sound of trickling water, the water simply gushed out of a broken pipe into a drain. I decided that as I could not spare the time and money to install a proper drain, it could remain as was for another fifty years, if the house remained upright for that long!

Putting up wallboard was equally frustrating. In most houses the wall studs were supposed to be 16" apart. In ours, finding one was a matter of guesswork. I would hammer in a nail only to hit thin air and there would be a series of holes before I struck pay dirt. Realizing that our house on Amphion Steet would never make the pages of the "Better Homes of British Columbia," I gave up the battle and allowed wear and tear caused by boisterous children, to reduce the place to what some people liked to call "A house with character!" I called it something else. But like our previous house it provided a shelter of sorts, and strangely enough my children now speak of it as being a home of happy memories. Our house was popular with other children in the neighbourhood because they were able to play the sort of games in it that their parents would not have allowed in their own homes. Stories began to circulate in the dockyard that I had bought a ramshackle house and that if an earthquake were to hit the area it would collapse. These stories were completely without foundation.

On one occasion I returned from a lengthy absence at sea and found that a hole larger than a football had been made in a bedroom wall. In a fit of pique I covered it with a sheet of cardboard, making no attempt to make a nice fit. And to demonstate to the children that I no longer cared how the rooms looked, I told them to cut-out dozens of attractive, coloured pictures from Life and other magazines. We pasted these scraps of paper with a flour and water glue, and covered the entire walls with Hollywood stars, shiny new cars, bandits, gangsters, exotic animals, and anything that looked good. It was a success.

Feeling in a reckless mood and dissatisfied with the outside appearance of the house, I decided to paint it. It was a decision I was to regret when half way through the job. I had yet to learn that preparation takes more time than the painting. Peeling paint had to be removed, a tedious business when done with a scraper particularly in the hard to reach places. Holes had to be plugged and areas around windows had to be taped if the job was to be done properly. I had visions of transforming the ugly old structure into an object of glistening beauty; a place I could be proud of. This vision turned into a mirage and the longer I toiled the more I began to realize that my dream had turned into an optical delusion.

The trickiest part was painting the apex at the front of the house about 45 feet high and beyond the reach of my heavy, forty foot, wooden ladder. The only way to reach it was from above, which meant climbing onto the roof, on which I was unable to stand, due to the steep pitch. To overcome this difficulty I had to practice some seamanship by using a rope. I secured this to the chimney further up the roof and passed it around my waist rather like a bosun's chair. I made the line fast in such a way that I was able to slack it if needed. And so I was able to reach the hitherto unreachable and with a few swift and none too skilful flourishes with the 4" brush, the job was complete. I descended to the ground to take a look at the fruits of many hours of labour and looked up. The result was discouraging. "You cannot make a silk purse out of a sow's ear."

7

The *Oshawa*

I was sent to the "*Oshawa*", an ex-naval vessel. She had twin screws powered by steam reciprocating engines which gave her a speed of 16 knots. A most uncomfortable ship when running at full speed in a rough sea, as the vibration was such that making legible entries in the log book was almost impossible. Anyone trying to decipher the scribble would have given up. It was the first time I had given orders to the helmsman through a voice-pipe as he was steering the ship from the deck below. Standing in the wheelhouse of this vessel in rough weather, one could hardly communicate due to the terrific clatter made by steel against steel, the rush of air through pipes and ventilators, and the crash of seas at her bows. She had a curious and nauseating motion when steaming into a head sea; a half pitch, half rolling plunge which was enough to send me and a few others, to the ships side to lay ground bait for fish. After a week of this it was a relief to enter the Juan de Fuca Strait and drop anchor in San Juan harbour.

Some of the seamen felt the need to get away from the ship for a few hours. A motor boat was lowered and I volunteered to take it away with a crew of ten men. Feeling in an adventurous mood, I steered for the head of the bay and into the San Juan River. At first it was an enjoyable trip as we motored up the winding river past densely wooded banks, but as it became narrower our progress was hindered by the debris of fallen trees; I decided to turn around. I had failed to notice that the tide was rushing out and soon we touched bottom. With the dreaded prospect of being stranded half a mile up river until the next tide I ordered everyone over the side to shove the two ton boat into deeper water. After much exertion this was accomplished and with a huge sense of relief we got clear of the river, and out into the bay. Back aboard I had time to ponder the tricky tidal problems of coastal navigation.

36

8

The Whitethroat

In 1961 I was promoted to 2nd mate of the *Whitethroat*. She was an Isle class trawler built in 1944 in Beverley, Yorkshire, England. She was 176 feet long and powered by a steam reciprocating engine. Transferred to the Canadian Navy the *Whitethroat* came to the West Coast in 1944 for the use of the Pacific Naval Laboratory. She carried a civilian crew of about twenty men plus six marine scientists known to us as "buggies." With this number of people aboard, living conditions were crowded. The master's and mate's accommodation was near the bridge. An additional house had been added abaft the funnel to accommodate the scientists and chief engineer. The crew's quarters were in the fore part of the ship below the main deck in what was formerly a cable tank. They reached it through a small hatch on the main deck.

'Whitethroat'
Living conditions were cramped but she was a good sea boat.

I shared a pokey cabin in the stern with the 3rd mate. Being the senior mate I claimed the bottom bunk. This cabin was situated next to the officers' wardroom. To reach this accommodation, one had to enter a hole in the deck and climb down a ladder. The 2nd and 3rd engineer lived next door. The 3rd engineer was a big man of advanced years who had difficulty squeezing through the hole, particularly after a heavy meal. I would hear him wheezing and grunting as he heaved his massive bulk onto the ladder and through the hole. I wondered whether he might have an attack of some kind and plug it for good.

None of the spaces in this compartment had port holes because it was below the waterline. Whatever ventilation there was, it did little to circulate the stale air and the only escape in the event of an emergency was via the small hatch. If ever there was a death trap aboard ship, this was it. In effect most of the crew lived below the ship's waterline. It was cramped and uncomfortable living quarters especially in rough weather, but there was one thing in the *Whitethroat's* favour, she was a good sea boat, strongly built from a well tested North Sea trawler design.

I was pleased to have the responsibility of being the ship's navigator, but in such a small wheelhouse it was a challenging job. With the ship plunging about in heavy seas off the West Coast, fixing her position had its hazards. She was equipped with one of the earliest Loran sets (DAS-1) situated on a ledge less than 3 feet from where the quartermaster stood at the wheel. When operating this Loran, I would sit on a stool which placed my backside perilously close to the spinning spokes of the wheel. When the ship rolled to port, my stool would slide in that direction and the spokes of the turning wheel came close to disemboweling me.

When I was seasick, which was usually the case, the operation of DAS-I was an exercise in endurance. It was performed in three phases, the selection of a signal which jumped up and down on a green background, (an appropriate colour.) The exact super-imposing of two, ever moving sine waves was necessary, and finally, the reading from this wretched instrument. I would then try to plot our position on the Loran chart, folded several times to fit on the chart table, only to find, that it was nowhere near our dead reckoning position. There were three likely reasons for this; one, I had incorrectly read the loran signal, two, the signal was too weak to read properly and I was apt to guess, or three, because the chart table was so positioned that only a skilled contortionist could use it with ease. No wonder its awkwardness sometimes effected the accuracy of my navigation.

In command was Captain MacDuff, a stoutish man in his late fifties, with a sad face and sallow complexion. He gave the distinct impression that he was not happy with his job. He never spoke about his past, but the story was that he had spent many years on China coasters. He seldom laughed and never joked. To the crew he was known as "Smiler." When at sea he had a passion for fixing the ship's position even when we were on station and stopped. He would come to the bridge at the most unexpected times and order" Get me a fix and a cup of tea." This became something of a joke aboard and ashore when members of the crew were in the Tudor House pub and gave the same command to the barman.

Captain Mac took great pleasure in doing things in the traditional manner. Things like radar and loran were useful, but if there was one instrument aboard to best demonstrate skill in navigation it was the sextant. Many men attached great reverence and almost magical properties to this. I remember seamen whose greatest desire was to learn how to use a sextant. Holding a sextant firmly in one's hand seemed to imply a certain authority, and certainty that the ship was in safe hands. The fact that a chronometer, a nautical almanac, and a book of tables were necessary to fix the position did not occur to them. They thought that Latitude and Longitude were read directly from the sextant.

There was evidently a good deal of one-upmanship played among certain seamen. There were those who could take a sight and those who couldn't, and those who didn't give a damn anyway. With Captain Mac, proficiency with a sextant was the ultimate accolade, and he would come to the bridge wielding his "hambone" as if it were a magic wand. It was like a great actor's prop and he handled it with reverence. It was the sort of thing that some deep-sea men liked to do in front of coastal men who may have felt lost when 30 miles offshore. Aboard the Whitethroat plotting our noon position was the highlight of the day. A ritual performed by some officers acting with the devoutness of a priest giving communion. There was an atmosphere of high drama in the wheelhouse, when the person privileged to make the mark on the chart announced that this was indeed our noon position. This done they could then return to more mundane duties.

The captain seemed to prefer being at sea to life ashore. After two or three weeks at sea off the West Coast the crew were very happy when the chief scientist announced that his work was complete and we could return to the base. It was my job to measure the distance and give the radio officer our estimated time of arrival. This was sent to the naval headquarters in Esquimalt. Sometimes we made better speed than estimated, and to everyone's delight (except the captain) we expected to reach port an hour or two earlier than first estimated. The crew were infuriated when the captain, not wanting to lose face by having to amend our E.T.A, ordered a reduction of speed in order that we would arrive in port when he said we would.

9

A storm at Station Poppa

In January 1962, Captain Robert Hooper took command of the *Whitethroat*. He was a tall, youthful man in his forties who liked to keep his distance from the crew. This was not easy on a small ship. Our first trip of the year was to Station "Poppa" where the Canadian Weather ship *Stonetown* steamed in a grid for a period of five weeks until relieved by her sister ship. She was stationed 900 miles west of the Straits of Juan de Fuca. The scientists aboard the *Whitethroat* wanted to stop at certain positions on the way so that they could take samples of water at various depths, this was called a "Line P." Among the instruments in the laboratory on the main deck was the Edo sounding machine which was capable of recording depths of more than 3000 fathoms.

On reaching a position along the Line, the ship was stopped, a wire was then lowered from a small davit into the water and Nansen bottles were attached at various intervals on the wire. When the desired depth was reached, a tripping device was sent down the wire to activate the lids on the bottles and collect water samples. It was tedious work. We had made several week-long trips with the same group of scientists, but this one was different because they were unable to do any work due to bad weather. Most of them remained horizontal, paralysed by sea sickness.

After the scientific work had been completed, we left Esquimalt with six scientists, and two bags of mail to be delivered to the Weather ship Stonetown (an ex naval frigate). Despite the physical discomforts, life aboard the *Whitethroat* was tolerable because we had a congenial crew. The mate was Gordon Cockroft, a cheerful fellow who had served his time with the Booth Line of Liverpool. He was skilled in every aspect of seafaring, had all the qualifications and should have been in command of a ship, however he was too easy-going and preferred to remain where he was. I remember Gordon with affection. Whenever the discomforts of life aboard a crowded ship plunging wildly in a turbulent sea became hard to bear, he had the ability to make light of it. He never became rattled by the angry rantings of unhappy men who hated being at sea. He was contented, saying " It is a great life if you don't weaken."

At 2330 hrs, I was roused by a shout from a seaman telling me that it was time to go on watch, and that the weather was foul. We had only just entered the Juan de Fuca Straits, yet already there was an unpleasant motion as the ship plunged into an increasingly heavy westerly swell. After a prolonged stay in port I had lost my sea legs. I would have to endure a few days of mal de mer before regaining them. Knowing that an uncomfortable watch lay ahead, I struggled into the warmest clothing I could find. While suppressing the inevitable onslaught of sea sickness and foregoing the usual cup of tea, I climbed out of the hole and staggered on deck to be greeted by a cold shower of spray. In the wheelhouse the 3rd mate, Michael Dyer, was balanced on a stool, propped against the binnacle. He was one of the great immune, but he didn't brag about it, handing over the watch to me and slipping quietly away to his bunk.

The quartermaster on my watch was Dennis Malarno. He was a fellow with an irrepressible sense of humour, except in rough weather when his constant chatter ceased, his face went white and he made frequent trips from the steering position to the ship's side. I liked Dennis if only because he was a fellow sufferer. On this trip we shared our common dilemma. As we steamed west the weather became progressively worse and Denis would call out " Hey there second mate, take the wheel please." I knew what he wanted and didn't need a second bidding. I grabbed the helm and watched as he crouched wretchedly over the lee rail spewing his supper into the wild night.

We were well out into the Pacific Ocean before the chief scientist appeared in the wheelhouse, pale and disheveled. He didn't need to be told that sea conditions made it impractical to stop the ship so that he and his associates could take water samples. Still we pressed on. Anyone who has spent a lengthy time aboard a small vessel in heavy weather knows how physically exhausting it is, for one is constantly bracing oneself against the violent movement of the ship.

When on watch I would strive to find a place in the wheelhouse where I could wedge myself between solid objects, and, with my legs splayed out in such a way as to prevent being thrown heavily into an empty space. The helmsman had a difficult job in a seaway trying to keep the ship on course while remaining on his feet. He stood on a wooden grating and sometimes a particularly heavy roll would send him and the grating sliding across the deck. Of course everything moveable had been stowed away securely, but because the chart table was in a fore and aft position the drawers were apt to slide out and onto the deck

Meal times were difficult for those with any inclination to eat. The man with the most unenviable job aboard was the cook. I remember cooks who received no thanks for their efforts to produce a decent meal in trying conditions, and I knew some who didn't deserve thanks. But our cook was a man who did his best and we appreciated it. He toiled in a small galley over an oil stove on which pots and pans were secured from shifting by steel bars. The crew's meals had to be carried from the galley along the open deck and lowered down to their messroom below the fore deck. The messman delivering it in stormy conditions had to be agile and quick if the food was to arrive hot on the table.

Our messman was a bright and cheerful kid who earlier had the misfortune to lose his right hand in an accident. The hand was replaced with a steel claw and he could use it with remarkable dexterity. Whenever a seaman gave him a hard time the messman had a novel way of getting his own back. When serving food to the crew he would pick up a plate, which was too hot to handle, with his claw, and give it to his tormentor! Food destined for the officer's mess was sent via a dumb waiter, which in rough weather had a tendency to jam when a load of food was half way between the decks. In an effort to free it, the mess steward would then shake the wire vigorously This caused a sudden drop, a heap of broken crockery and a mess of food.

After three days of hard steaming we arrived at Station "Poppa" during the hours of darkness. We were now hove-to in a howling gale and heavy sea. The lights of the Weather ship *Stonetown* were barely visible in the driving rain. There was no question of transferring mail until the weather moderated. It seemed a futile journey to have made, merely to deliver two bags of mail, when not one scientist had left his bunk to put a Nansen bottle over the side. During the middle watch I checked the barometer frequently. The pressure continued to fall and when the mate arrived at 0400 the reading was below 28 inches.

After two hours I was awakened from a restless sleep and was immediately aware that the ship's movement had now become violent. I had the feeling that whatever was going on outside I did not want to spend any more time down the hole. I wasn't the only one who felt that way. The 3rd engineer was on his way to the engine room. "What sort of weather have you deck wallas got us into now? Its crazy up there. This is no place for man nor beast. I should have taken sick leave before we sailed," he muttered as he disappeared through the hole.

On reaching the top of the ladder I looked across a sloping deck on to a turbulent sea. It was almost completely white. The wind was now so strong that as a wave broke in a tumbling mass of foam it was immediately followed by another steep and threatening sea.

The force of the wind and the violence of the pitching made progress on deck both difficult and dangerous. The canvas dodger, stretched across the bridge rail to protect us from the elements, was torn to ribbons. Grasping whatever was at hand, I crouched down in an effort to resist the onslaught and fought my way to the wheelhouse where a worried looking *old man* was talking to the chief engineer. "Chief, I want every ounce of steam you've got. She keeps on wanting to fall-off course. We have to put the wheel hard over to bring her back. If the steering gear fails and we come beam-on to this sea, we've had it!" It is not often that the master of a ship makes a statement of that kind. The chief engineer left the wheelhouse. No doubt he was worried about his machinery. We were in dire straits. If the main engine failed or the steering gear broke down, the ship would be at the mercy of the elements

Any queasiness I felt earlier was now replaced by unease of another kind. The view ahead of the ship was a daunting one. During the war I had seen big seas from the bridge of a 14,000 ton tanker off the Cape of Good Hope; they were following seas, about fifty feet high and generated by westerly gales. The great North Pacific rollers which the 800 ton *Whitethroat* was now heading into were all of that and more. An anemometer (wind gauge) was fitted at the truck of our mast, and its cups were now whirring around like a plane's propeller. It was registering wind gusts of 90 knots but remarkably, when we lay in the trough (the hollow between waves) a huge sea rose up like a wall ahead of us and the four cups on the anemometer were almost motionless. The mast was 60 feet above the sea. A wave of that height or more, was momentarily sheltering the ship from the wind!

But the *Whitethroat* was a well built ship and her steam engine never missed a beat. She brought us through a bad blow. After a 12 hour battering, the wind began to subside and the seas became less precipitous. We spoke to the *Stonetown* six miles away. She hadn't weathered the storm as well as we had, having been pushed back 2 miles in 24 hrs, whereas we had made 1 mile headway! Thus a trip lasting ten days had achieved nothing. The crew on the weather ship didn't get their mail, and the "buggies" aboard the *Whitethroat* remained in their bunks. No meals were served for two days, for the cook had long since given up cooking as conditions made it almost impossible. We were fed sandwiches and apples, not all of which was digested. Three days later we returned to port and some welcome time at home.

Captain Rob Macdonald was a man with whom it was a pleasure to sail. He was in command of the *Whitethroat* when we sailed north through the inland passage into Alaskan waters, on a trip lasting three weeks. I cannot remember the purpose of this voyage, but it was an enjoyable one. We steamed at a leisurely speed as there were no commercial restraints to prevent the captain from taking time to stop in a sheltered bay, drop the anchor, lower a boat and go fishing. We ventured into remote and lonely inlets in Alaska, places where ships seldom went. Punchbole Inlet was one I remember as being particularly beautiful.

Only one incident marred my enjoyment of the trip. We had anchored in a bay near the open ocean. The mate wanted to take the boat out to look at the sea lions lying on rocks nearby. I went with him and later wished that I stayed aboard. I didn't know that he had a rifle in the boat and intended to use it. He took the boat as close to the rocks as he could, stopped the engine, then stood up and began shooting the sea lions. The rocks were covered with blood as the poor beasts fell into the sea. Disgusted by this wanton cruelty, I asked him to stop. He ignored me, saying that he was only doing fishermen a favour as sea lions ate too many fish. I was glad when he soon ran out of ammunition.

On one trip we carried a group of Zoologists from the University of British Columbia who wanted to gather marine life from the Straits of Georgia. We dragged their equipment along the seabed, then it was raised and the contents dumped on the deck. The 'buggies' examined it with great enthusiasm. There were oohs and aahs when a particular specimen caught their interest and it would be taken into the laboratory for further study under a microscope. The seaman considered this fuss over a heap of sludge, rather amusing. They were bored with the operation, and one of them had mischief in mind to enliven the daily routine.

At noon the scientists knocked -off for lunch. Spinach was on the menu and the prankster went to the galley, grabbed a handful, and threw it on the heap of debris which had recently been raised from the deep. He then hid behind the deck house to watch the fun. On returning to work the scientists examined the heap of debris and soon there was cries of excitement as one of them picked up the spinach. They were unable to identify it and thinking that they had made a significant discovery the spinach was taken to the lab. The chief scientist was called and for several minutes there was close consultation among them. The chief scientist was frowning when he emerged from the lab holding the spinach. " Who is responsible for this?" he shouted. " We have wasted time and I will speak to the captain." The old man did not like being disturbed from his afternoon siesta, but promised to look into the matter. Of course we all knew who was responsible and so did the old man, but he had other things to think about, and the matter was forgotten.

10

Assistance not required

The *Whitethroat* was sent on various trips out into the Pacific Ocean with parties of scientists. These trips were usually routine and dull because we had no particular destination, so when something out of the ordinary occurred it was a welcome diversion. On one occasion we were obliged to seek shelter from a gale and dropped anchor in a secluded cove in Nootka Sound. It was late in the evening when Sparks received a message saying that a fishing boat had been driven ashore and wrecked. The boat's lone occupant had managed to send a May Day and it was presumed he was alive but marooned on the beach. We looked at the chart and saw that we were the closest ship to the site of the wreck, but as the gale was still raging, it would be quite impractical to attempt a rescue from the sea. It was decided to wait until dawn and send a shore party to walk through the forest to the coast, a distance of about three miles. A party of four seamen set off at dawn. It was cold and wet, but fortified by a hearty breakfast they set off for the nearby beach and we watched them step ashore and disappear into the dense bush.

When they had not returned by noon the *old man* became concerned. Surely a short hike through the bush to rescue a distressed fisherman would take no more than four or five hours. As the hours dragged by there was discussion as to whether a message should be sent to naval headquarters to send out another rescue party to retrieve the rescuers. Late in the afternoon the party was seen on the beach and a boat was sent ashore to pick them up. They had had a rough time, and were bruised, scratched and exhausted.

After a meal and medical attention they told their story. Anyone who has tried to walk through the dense forest of coastal British Columbia in mid-winter knows that it is not like an easy, casual stroll in the country. At first they made good progress, it was fun. There was shouts of laughter as they scrambled over dead trees, pushed their way past tangled vines, and made ribald remarks when the irrepressible Dennis Maluarno tripped over a log and disappeared into a water filled ditch. After two hours of strenuous plodding they began to tire. Instead of joking they began to curse, then fell silent. They worried whether they were heading in the right direction.

It was a great relief when they heard the sound of waves crashing ashore, and moments later they stumbled out of the bush onto the beach. Fortunately their navigation had been accurate. They sighted a wreck out in the surf and on the beach nearby a heap of wood taken from the wreck shaped to form a shelter from which, to their amazement, a cloud of smoke rose. Dennis, in a state of near exhaustion, addressed the heap of wood " Bloody hell, I don't believe it! Is anyone in here?" There was movement from within the shelter, then a small wiry man with a cigarette in his mouth emerged. His clothes were dry and he appeared in excellent condition. "Goddam, who the hell are you?" "We have come to rescue you" said Dennis weakly. The fisherman laughed. "Rescued, what for? I'm alright." When told that he must accompany them through the bush to the *Whitethroat*, he relit his fag and said, "That's crazy. Why would I do that?" He was quite comfortable as he was and would wait until the weather moderated, help would arrive from along the beach, or he would walk to the nearest coastal settlement.

His rescuers were somewhat put out by his lack of appreciation for their efforts, and now they had to face a rough hike back through the bush with nothing to show for it. And so the sorry episode ended when the bedraggled, intrepid, bad-tempered rescuers came back aboard again. An entry in the ship's log noted that " Fisherman located by rescue party. Assistance not required. Party returned aboard." They could have added " Much the worse for wear too."

11

Pulling the plug on the *Whitethroat*

"Their want of practice will make them unskilful, and their want of skill timid. Maritime skill like skills of another kind, is not to be cultivated by the way, or at chance times"
.
                                        Thucydides. 460-400 B.C.

Recent proverb: "A man who does nothing never makes a mistake".
                                          A.F.W. 1966 A.D.

Dr. Barry was an Oceanographer from the University of British Columbia. He specialized in the magnetics branch of this science. He was a New Zealander with one hand missing but he was as dexterous as anyone with two hands. He usually had an assistant to help with the equipment, particularly the magnetometer which was lowered over the side and towed at varying speeds. On this occasion we were operating in the calm waters of the Saanich Inlet near Victoria. It was tedious work for the mates; hours spent on the bridge running up and down the Inlet until Dr Barry was satisfied with a day's work, and then we would return to the dock at Patricia Bay and tie-up for the night.

It was quiet and peaceful during my afternoon watch. For those not on watch it was siesta time. The *old man*, the mate and 3rd mate had all retired to their bunks, only Dr Barry, his assistant and the seaman on watch were on deck. I was on the bridge when the phone rang. It was Dr. Barry. "Tony, I have finished for today, we can go back to the dock."

Before calling the *old man* and putting the engine-room telegraph on stand-by, I had a certain duty to perform. We were equipped with an instrument known as a Chernerkiff Log which was necessary to determine our speed as accurately as possible. It was located in a compartment (void space) directly below the crew's messroom. When in operation the Chernerkiff log projected about a foot below the hull.

It was a sword-like apparatus housing a brass impeller which was turned by the ship's forward movement. This was connected electrically to dials (registering speed and distance) in the laboratory and wheelhouse. Before going alongside the dock the log had to be lifted inboard to prevent possible damage to the impeller. This was a simple operation, I had performed it many times. Armed with a crescent wrench and a flashlight, I went down into the crew's messroom, lifted the manhole cover and descended about eight feet into the complete darkness of the void tank. There were two nuts on either side of the log. The two outer nuts held the flange in place on the ship's hull, the two inner nuts held the log in the "in" or "out" position.

As was usually the case, I was in a hurry to lift the log and speed-up our return to the dock. Setting the wrench to the right size, I reached down and in rapid succession slackened two nuts. There was a loud swoosh as water gushed in with incredible force and soon covered my ankles. A sudden terror gripped me and with visions of coming to a premature end inside the tank, I dashed to the ladder, scrambled out, slammed the cover shut and secured it. It was done in record time. Realizing that I had slackened the wrong nuts, I stood for a while sweating, cursing and contemplating the consequences of my carelessness.

On reporting to Captain Hooper that his command was in some danger of sinking, I expected a terrific blast, but none came. His face turned white, but with commendable composure he remained silent for a moment. Losing a ship at sea is one thing, but foundering half a mile from land in a protected inlet? Captain Hooper could have been contemplating either murder, or suicide. But all was not lost, by good fortune he had a friend who was a frogman living nearby. Radio contact was made, a boat was hurriedly launched and within half an hour he was aboard. Donning his wet suit and mask, the frogman entered the tank and secured the nuts. The water was pumped out and the *Whitethroat* was declared seaworthy once more.

News of my attempt to scuttle a unit of her Majesty's Pacific Fleet soon reached rumour-mongers in the Dockyard. I expected severe repercussions from the High Command, but none came. Oddly enough I got the distinct impression that in some circles at least, my reputation was much enhanced by this audacious escapade.

Possibly the authorities had punishment in mind when I was banished to the tug St Anthony, for if ever there was a purgatory afloat, it was this vessel. She was powered by two Fairbanks Morse diesels and capable of 16 knots. When viewed from a distance she appeared modern and somewhat rakish. Indeed almost everything aboard her had a rake. The funnel, masts, wheelhouse and most of all the main deck sloped towards the stern. This is called sheer (the upward sweep from amidships to forward and aft of a vessel's freeboard deck), and it was so pronounced in the St Anthony that standing a bridge watch and fighting to remain perpendicular was a debilitating experience. It was akin to standing on the slope of a mountain, difficult enough in calm weather, almost impossible in a rough head sea.

She was a terrible sea boat, as I was about to discover, when we sailed for Kodiac, Alaska via Astoria, Washington. Even in a moderate sea the after deck was constantly awash and heavy weather made it an unsafe area. When buffeted by a head sea, visibility was effected by the constant spray over the bridge. The bow would rise steeply to a heavy sea, but not quickly enough to reach the crest and there was a heavy thump as a green roller came aboard and the entire vessel was enveloped in solid water. It was a roller coaster of a ride as she plunged down into the trough of a steep sea and then lifted her bows sharply to climb up the next one. This was the sort of lively behavior to bring on an attack of mal de mer to anyone with a weak stomach such as myself.

The reason for our going to Astoria escapes me. It may have been to collect scientific equipment, on the other hand it might have been a trip merely to justify the vessel's and our existence. The trip south was relatively comfortable as the wind and sea were astern of us, but when we headed north for Alaska the seas were rough. The ship was awash for a week, swept by seas which came over the bow with such consistency that the horizon was only visible for brief periods between the deluges. Meal times were awkward. When I sat down in the messroom I found that my chin was level with the edge of the table. This was due to excessive camber(arched form of the deck to shed water) and I had to sit on a lifejacket in order to reach my food. Although true to form I often felt too sick to face any refreshment.

51

After a week of discomfort we entered the U.S. Navy air base. This was situated on what appeared to be a barren island for there was little vegetation. There was no incentive to go ashore except to make a phone call but for some of us the cost of telling the folks back home how much we missed them, was too high. After a month's absence we were glad to return to the serenity of the dockyard.

There were days when I watched the naval ships steam out of Esquimalt harbour bound for exercises with the U.S. Navy in Hawaiian waters, and I longed for an ocean voyage to some distant shores. For sailors of the Pacific Fleet a cruise to the balmy waters off Hawaii was generally regarded as an escape from the frustration and tedium of life in the Dockyard. For me the boredom of inactivity at work was compounded by frustrations of life ashore. The house needed repairs but there was never enough money to pay for the materials. During my pre-dockyard days whenever I did have money, I never had the time to make repairs. Now that I had the time I did not have the money.

I made a request to be transferred back to the *Whitethroat*. To my surprise it was granted. There was great excitement aboard when we were ordered to prepare for a trip to San Francisco and San Diego. It was winter time in Victoria so the oceanographers had found a good reason to do some research work in the balmy waters of Southern California. I ordered charts and enjoyed plotting the courses for this voyage into warmer climes. Extra stores were ordered, and as the climate of Southern California can be hot, we thought we should rig an awning over the after deck. One was ordered, but this original idea was shot-down by the master who was anxious to avoid any unnecessary expense. He went to the superintendent and gave him a hundred reasons why we should not go south and none for making the trip. One would have thought we were off on a voyage around the world! I did have the pleasure of obtaining the charts, even though it was only a voyage down the coast and back.

It proved to be an enjoyable jaunt into warmer waters. We stopped at San Francisco en route. Those with the financial resources were able to go ashore and sample the various diversions available there. In San Diego one of our seamen was arrested for being drunk and disorderly; I was sent to bail him out. He was extremely pleased to see me and shook my hand, saying that he would never complain again about conditions aboard the ship. He had spent a terrible night in the company of murderers, con artists, petty thieves, and men who had unwholesome designs on his person. Board and lodging cost him $100, which was deducted from his wages.

The scientists had work to do about thirty miles south of San Diego but we had some difficulty fixing the ship's position. This seemed a bit odd when we were so close to the largest naval base on the Pacific Coast. It wasn't possible to use a sextant as the skies were overcast and we were too far off the coast of Mexico to fix our position by shore bearings or radar. The only means left was our primitive loran. The Mexican Government had refused to allow a station to be located on its territory, and as we were too close to the loran base line we were unable to get a fix. We were left to plot our position by dead reckoning.

There must have been times when the Naval Authorities back in Ottawa were wondering whether much work was being done in the Esquimalt Dockyard. Ugly rumours about a permanent slow-down may have filtered back east. In 1964 the ships of the auxiliary fleet were ordered to make a Time and Motion study. Translated this meant that all hands had to account for their activities during a working day. When the *old man* mentioned this directive at the coffee break, and produced a piece of paper to prove he wasn't joking, there was a stunned silence. This was a challenge to a man's professional pride. It had to be met with convincing proof of industry aboard ship even if it wasn't very evident ashore. Each man had to complete a form which showed what he was doing during 15 minute intervals of an eight day shift. It was difficult to take this seriously, and after some of us attempted to fill the form with spurious information we eventually abandoned the exercise, and returned to work.

12

The *Laymore* in distress!

I was at home one weekend, when an urgent call came from the office of the Queen's Harbourmaster. The *Laymore* was in trouble and the tug *Clifton* was being readied to go to her assistance. She needed a 2nd mate. I packed my bag and hurried to the dockyard. The *Laymore* had been laid-up for months. She was no longer needed now that the *Endeavour* was operational. Her stores were taken off, her crew sent elsewhere, and for some unknown reason her two propellers were removed. There must have been a lack of communication between certain naval authorities because not all obsolete depth charges had been disposed of. There was evidently some urgency to do this and the *Laymore*, even minus her propellers, was considered the only vessel suitable for this operation.

Naval experts got their collective heads together and considered the possibility of loading the shells onto a barge and towing it to the dumping area. This proposal was rejected by a Lieutenant Bird who ordered that the *Laymore* should do the job. She would be manned by her usual crew, loaded with shells and towed by the tug *Heatherington*. Naturally this hare-brained scheme was greeted with derision in some quarters. Experienced tug masters said it was both unwise and possibly dangerous to tow a "dead" ship carrying explosives and with a crew aboard. But the *Heatherington* with the *Laymore* in tow was ordered to sea, and once clear of Cape Flattery they ran into a full gale and heavy seas. The master of the tug had the safety of his own vessel to consider and when conditions became worse he was forced to slip the tow and leave the *Laymore* to wallow in the heavy swells.

One can appreciate the dilemma facing the master of a powerless, ammunition laden ship in storm conditions. She was beam-on to the elements and her rolling was so violent that it was almost impossible for her hapless crew to stand. Later I spoke to one of her seaman. He said that some of the men were terrified and were lying prostrate on the deck. The master instructed the radio officer to transmit a Mayday and ordered the crew to abandon ship. The crew had difficulty in getting into the inflatable liferaft. It was reported that one man was so paralysed by fear that it took the combined strength of two seamen to force him to release his grip on a rail and push him into the raft floating alongside. All the crew got clear of the ship in one raft. They were now dry and warm but the violence of the motion was such that every man was terribly sick.

A Canadian naval destroyer was dispatched to the scene and steamed at full speed into a heavy sea. She pounded so roughly that the sonar dome on her bow was torn off, but the captain pressed on and was soon at the scene. By skilful seamanship he manoeuvered his ship to make a lee and every man was rescued.

After hard steaming at our best speed of about six knots we arrived on the scene at daybreak. The weather had moderated but there was still a heavy swell running. A number of frogmen from the destroyer had managed to board the *Laymore* and after some difficulty a line was passed to us and we towed her back to Esquimalt.

13

To the Okanagan by Dodge and back by Ford

After four years in Victoria my family and I felt badly in need of a holiday even though we really couldn't afford one. We had been forced to manage without a holiday when our two youngest children had arrived; Stephanie was born in 1960 and Vincent in 1962, and the desire to own a means of transport was overwhelming. I began to search for a car which would carry two adults and nine children. It's cost would have to come within our limited means. I voiced this need in the wardroom of the *Oshawa*, a vessel to which I had been sent for a short time. The 3rd engineer had just the right car for me, or so it seemed at the time. It was a Dodge station wagon about ten years old. It appeared to be in good condition and feeling that I had got a real bargain I paid $700 for it. This was a big mistake and a costly one, and I should have known better. It was not a good idea to buy an old car from a shipmate, who seemed over anxious to explain all the advantages to be gained by owning it.

It was summer time and I was entitled to two weeks leave, but after buying the car we were short of cash, and it would have been wise to have stayed at home. However the children having been promised a holiday showed signs of revolt. It would have to be a holiday on the cheap.

We set off for the Okanagan with a full load; two adults, nine kids, plus a recently acquired full grown Labrador. For the reader who might wonder how so many souls could fit into a station wagon? I can only say that I sometimes wonder about that myself. We reached the town of Hope, 100 miles from Vancouver, in the afternoon and put up for the night at a motel on Sultan Lake. No sooner had we settled in after a swim in the lake when a storm arrived and heavy rain drove us to take shelter. Early next morning, we began the long climb up the Hope-Princeton Highway. Our spirits were high. Kelowna was only another 200 miles away.

We hadn't gone far before the wretched clutch began to slip badly and I knew that we would never reach the summit. At least it was a downhill run back to Hope in search of a service station, but it was Saturday and there was no hope of any repairs until Monday. After the clutch was replaced, at a cost of $60, my initial optimism about the holiday began to wilt a little and our troubles were far from over. We were about 20 miles from Penticton and about to descend the long hill into the town when an ominous thumping noise came from the engine. I bit my lip in effort to curb any outpouring of obscenities, and gently eased the car to the first service station we came to.

I was all for abandoning the vehicle as so much junk, but surprisingly a young mechanic at the service station offered $60 for it. I was quick to accept his generous offer before he changed his mind. Oddly enough it was the new roof rack which he needed most of all. And as that had cost $40 I felt pleased to have recovered some of my money.

The kids were not in the least discouraged by these setbacks. They were happy after the mechanic took us to the beach on Lake Kalamalka, where we pitched our tent and went for a swim. The weather was glorious and it looked as though we might have some fun after all.

The next day there was a sudden drop in temperature from 85 degrees F. to 45 degrees and this was followed by a hail storm. I never have enjoyed living in a tent and this onslaught was the final straw. I announced to all, that as far as I was concerned, the holiday was over. We packed up our belongings, I walked a mile into the town and rented a brand new Ford. We returned home to Victoria in some style and comfort.

There was still a problem. The Ford had to be returned. I needed a companion for the long drive back to Penticton and my eldest son, Andrew, was pleased to accompany me. After returning the car, we hopped on a bus to Kelowna where kind relations welcomed us. My uncle took us fishing on Lake Okanagan and we caught a few fish. We spent two happy days but with a seriously depleted wallet I wondered how we were going to get home. There was only one way to get there; we would hitch hike. We were driven to the outskirts of Kelowna and within minutes were picked up by a charitable driver. We were on our way. Three more lifts and six hours later we were in Vancouver. The rest was easy.

14

The *Endeavour*

The years spent in the Dockyard were not entirely wasted. I knew that if I was to be promoted I had to get my Master's ticket. A golden opportunity presented itself when I learned that I would remain on pay while studying at the Navigation school in Vancouver. One way to live cheaply in that city was to stay at the Salvation Army Hostel. The Hostel was situated in a dismal, seedy section of town and I did not relish living there, but this only spurred me on to work as hard as possible in order to shorten my stay.

I was fortunate in having the company of an engineer from the Dockyard. George Hunter and I had been shipmates on the *Oshawa* and he was now studying for his Chief's ticket. He was not only a cheerful fellow, but good at mathematics. His room was next to mine and whenever I ran into difficulties he would come in, look at the problem and help me to solve it, saying, "Hell Tony, what would you do without the engine department?" After four months of extreme mental exertion (and one failure to pass the written exam) the happy day came when I emerged from the examiner's office with a master's ticket in my hand. However the satisfaction I felt was tempered by the thought that it had taken me ten years longer than my contempories to pass this exam.

Now that I had my master's ticket, I was promoted sooner than expected. A new research ship had been built and there was a lot of speculation among the men of the auxiliary fleet about the manning of this vessel. The *Endeavour* was a 1200 ton(gross), 220 ft. motor ship driven by twin Fairbanks Morse engines and capable of 16 knots. With her hull and superstructure painted white, and a domed shaped, buff coloured funnel she looked impressive. A lot was expected of her. She was fitted with some advanced technological improvements but some of these didn't work and she became something of a " White Elephant."

Captain MacDuff was appointed Master of the Endeavour. The mate, Ed Maloney, was a hardened old sea dog from Newfoundland. George Hunter, having got his ticket was the 2nd engineer and I was the 2nd mate. With the other officers, we gathered on the dock near the ship to attend the commissioning ceremony. The admiral of the base made a speech which was mercifully brief, and this was followed by one from " Smiler " who dropped his notes, and he had to improvise. This resulted in mumbled words into the microphone which were unintelligible. None of us were in the mood to listen anyway as there was a cold wind blowing, and our thoughts were on drinks in the wardroom once the ceremony was over.

'Endeavour'.
A research ship designed to be steady in rough sea..

Being a research ship it was important to ensure that the *Endeavour* was as steady as possible in rough seas. Bilge keels were not fitted as they tended to interfere with equipment put over the side. She was equipped with a flume tank, to reduce rolling, which was specially designed for the ship. This tank was partially filled with water, and as the ship began to heel, baffles prevented water from sloshing about. It was trapped on the high side thus dampening the roll.

It was a system that worked well in some ships when the rolling was reduced as much as 70%. It also had the advantage over the Denny-

Brown fin stabilizers which were only effective when the ship was under way, whereas the flume system worked when the ship was stopped. The flume system had been developed by the McMullen Institute of New York, but German and Milne the Canadian Naval Architects in Ottawa, being unwilling to pay for outside assistance in installing this system, decided to do the job themselves. They botched it.

Another feature in the construction of the *Endeavour*, to improve her steadiness at sea, was a bulbous bow. Unlike most bulbous bows, ours was shaped like a hammerhead shark. It was supposed to reduce pitching but it didn't work either.

After speed trials were run in calm waters, we sailed out into the Pacific Ocean to test the Flume tank and bulbous bow. Our instructions were to look for rough weather, stay in it and note how the systems worked. We didn't have to wait long. About 100 miles west of Cape Flattery we encountered a force 7 gale, rough seas and moderately heavy swell.

It's a pity that the designers of our flume tank and bulbous bow were not aboard, they may have been as surprised and uncomfortable as we were. I was on the afternoon watch when the ship began to heave and wallow in the most unpleasant and unexpected way. She would roll heavily, then there was a slight pause at the bottom of the roll, then she would flop over a bit more before righting herself. Of course it was the free-surface of a partially filled tank having the opposite of the desired effect. That was bad enough, now we had to test the bulbous bow.

The course was altered so that we were heading into the sea. We increased speed. The ship's bows rose steeply to meet a big wave, her fore-foot coming clean out of the water, then a downward plunge and terrific slam as she buried her bows in a mass of foam. The ship was shaken from stem to stern by the terrific impact. After a few minutes of this kind of punishment, the old man had seen enough. He was as alarmed as the rest of us and after making a few uncomplimentary remarks about the ship, and government naval architects in particular, he ordered an end to the test and we headed back to Esquimalt.

The *Endeavour* went into the drydock and it was no surprise to anyone that the bulbous bow was removed. The Flume System was abandoned, the space became a void tank, and no one with any sense mentioned them again.

'Endeavour'. The bulbous bow did not add to her steadiness in a rough sea.

'Endeavour' after her bulbous bow was removed.

In 1966 I was promoted to chief officer of the fleet oiler *Dundurn*. Although this meant an increase of wages I was not particularly elated. I had now been in the dockyard for eight years and was becoming increasingly restless. The thought of spending the rest of my working life in the torpid atmosphere surrounding the auxiliary fleet was too much to bear. At forty-six, surely I wasn't too old to change my job? I began to think of employment elsewhere.

Advertisements for ships' officers in the United States Military Sea Transportation Service began to appear in the classified sections of the local papers. The war in Vietnam had escalated and thousands of American soldiers were conscripted and being sent overseas. More ships were required to take them there. Mates and engineers were urgently required in the American Merchant Marine and it became necessary to recruit them from outside the country. The wages offered by the Americans were more than twice what I was earning in the dockyard.

On seeing this I felt a surge of excitement. This could be the very thing I needed. This sudden rush of optimism must have effected my behavior at home and my wife Celia wanted to know what it was all about. When I told her of my intentions to reply to the advertisement, she expressed doubt, saying, that it seemed too good to be true. " It is just a come on, they won't even answer your letter." This gloomy thought put a slight but temporary damper on my plans to leave the dockyard. I sent records of my sea service and references to the M.S.T.S. in Oakland, California; waited and hoped for the best.

During the next six anxious weeks there was a flurry of letters and phone calls. The M.S.T.S wanted to know more about me. They were obviously very particular about the people they enlisted. I began to have doubts, perhaps Celia was right and it was all a big lie. Rumours began to circulate in the dockyard about my impending departure and I cursed my folly for ever mentioning it to anyone. Now I would have to eat humble pie and accept the fact that once a man worked in the dockyard, it was for life, he wasn't wanted elsewhere. But when a letter arrived with instructions to proceed to California to be "Inducted into the M.S.T.S." all of those doubts were forgotten. I was elated.

My resignation from the dockyard was greeted with skepticism by some; "why would you give up a steady job like this?" said one mate, "Its crazy, think of your superannuation, you will lose it!" He spoke like a man talking to the condemned. "I didn't come to Canada to do this sort job." I replied smugly. "I feel as if I have one foot in the grave working here, and as for my superannuation, they can keep it, I'll take a chance elsewhere." Any doubts that I felt about leaving were dispelled by the ever cheerful Gordon Cockcroft whom I had sailed with on the *Whitethroat*. "I don't know of anyone who has left the dockyard and who hasn't been the better for it." he said, shaking my hand and wishing me luck. When I walked out of the gates for the last time, I felt no inclination to glance back.

15

Under the Stars and Stripes

Although the ships of the Military Sea Transportation Service were owned by the United States Navy, they were manned by merchant seamen under the jurisdiction of the Coast Guard, which ruled that a U.S. ship could carry foreign nationals as deck officers, but they could not be in charge of a watch at sea. According to the rules, the officer of the watch had to be an American subject and hold a Coast Guard license. The fact that I would not be in charge of the watch didn't bother me, it was more important to become used to the American way of running a ship. This would take time.

My first ship was the *Upshur*. She had been built in 1951 for the American President Lines of San Francisco, which ran a passenger and cargo service to the Far East, but she was taken over by the U.S. Navy after she was launched, and completed as a troopship. She was 12,000 gross tons and her geared turbines generated 13,000 h.p. driving a single propeller, and was capable of making 20 knots. Her complement was 2000 troops and a crew of about 180. She was a handsome ship with a rakish profile, the bridge being part of her tear shaped stack (funnel). Smoke from her boilers came out from two vent-posts abaft the stack.

I was one of three foreign mates aboard. We were to be assigned to each watch as juniors to assist the American officers. Our rank was 3rd officer. The other foreign mates were from Cuba and Britain; I was the only Canadian aboard. The Britisher was John Grey who had lived in California for many years. He had been in the British merchant service during the war, had recently been divorced and like me, was badly in need of money. He was an ill-tempered fellow who seemed intent on picking a fight with me. No matter what I said he would take exception to it, raising his voice as if to prove his point. He didn't like know-alls and I was one of the worst kind. "You should have stayed in bloody England, we don't want your kind here," he would say. When I told him that I was a Canadian he went on the offensive again, saying, "Well, that's where you should go back to." He hadn't come back to sea to be told how to do the job by the likes of a man like me. I realized that Grey had a problem, he had been ashore for over fifteen years and had probably forgotten most of what he had learned about the job.

Being anxious to settle down aboard, the last thing I wanted was to make enemies, but Grey was always in a belligerent mood. Matters came to a head when I told him that I had no intention of wasting time arguing, and suggested that he might like to take the matter further. For once he remained silent. The *Upshur* was a big ship with a large crew, there was room for both of us, and as we were on different watches there was no reason why we couldn't keep clear of each other during the coming voyage. During the following weeks I seldom set eyes on him, and when we did meet we never exchanged a word.

I felt sorry for Alberto the Cuban officer, he was a friendly fellow; but as he spoke very little English and none of us spoke Spanish, conversation was difficult. He appeared to be on his own and quite lost. How he managed to stand a bridge watch without being able to communicate, I do not know.

I had expected to be at sea shortly after joining the *Upshur* but she was undergoing repairs and we lay alongside the dock for a week. The accommodation for officers was spacious and comfortable. It was the first time I had been in air-conditioned accommodation, and I was enjoying the novelty of being aboard an American ship. After helping the chief officer make-up a muster list for lifeboat stations, I found time to explore the ship from stem to stern in an effort to become familiar with every part of her. This was interrupted when I was told to report to the medical department where I was vaccinated against cholera, typhoid, yellow fever and every other tropical disease known. I was jabbed in both arms, and the dosage was such that I was unable to lift my arms for two days.

In the evenings I was free to go ashore. I was pleased to be back in San Francisco again and renewed my friendship with the Colthurst family who lived in Fremont. They had been passengers aboard the 'Waikawa' on our voyage from Tahiti in 1951, when their son Rick was seven years old. He had been conscripted into the army and was now in Vietnam.

I was on the bridge when we steamed beneath the Golden Gate bridge bound for Okinawa. We were under the command of Captain Rhoades, a tall, stern, no nonsense captain who was far too busy to notice the arrival of a new mate aboard his ship. He relayed orders through the chief officer and never spoke to me during the voyage. There had been no time to obtain a khaki uniform and I felt out of place on the bridge in civilian clothes. When I asked the officer of the watch to be given a job, he seemed non-plussed and could only suggest that I stand aside and watch. This seemed the only sensible thing to do. Despite my initial feelings of inadequacy it was exhilarating to be aboard a large ocean going ship once again. I was now determined to prove to myself that I had not forgotten the duties of a watch-keeping officer, albeit aboard an American ship.

The *Upshur* was a fast ship and soon after the pilot was clear we were full away at a sea speed of 20 knots. Our passage was uneventful and after ten days we reached Naha the capital of the Okinawa Islands. We had come to pick up troops for Vietnam. The dock was jammed with army vehicles and soldiers ready to embark, each man with full pack, and no doubt wondering what lay ahead in the jungle. Our stay in Naha was brief. I wanted to mail some letters and see the town, having read of the fierce battle which took place when U.S. troops invaded the island in 1945. On my way back to the ship I got my first whiff of tear gas, and covered my nose with a handkerchief. A group of noisy demonstrators had confronted the police and their march towards the dock area was halted by a cloud of tear gas. It soon became evident that the presence of American troops was not popular among the people. A column of banner-holding protesters came towards the dock gates but their way was blocked by a line of police. The demonstrators dispersed.

En route to Vung Ro, Vietnam, we had reached the South China Sea and were approaching the coast of Vietnam. It was midnight. I was about to go off watch but stopped in the chartroom to watch the 2nd officer as he plotted our position. He told me that we would not cross the meridian which marked the danger zone until 15 minutes after midnight. Once in the zone, the entire ships crew of 235 men would get danger money, i.e. 100% increase of their wages. "To hell with it, why should we lose out on a day's extra bonus for a lousy 16 minutes? We will show that we were in the zone at 2345 hours. We

66

were in the zone on your watch. You can enter that in the log book."
The generosity of the navigating officer knew no bounds.

16

The *General Gordon*

On May 1st we were back in Oakland, California and I was transferred to the two funneled P.2.type troopship *General Gordon*. Built in 1944 in New Jersey by the Federal Shipbuilding Corporation, and designed to carry 3000 troops, the *General Gordon* was an impressive ship. She was of 18,000 gross tons, 622 ft long and a beam of 76 ft. driven by De Laval steam turbines of 19,000 h.p., and capable of 20 knots. She first saw action in the closing months of the war and visited ports in Europe, the Philippines and Japan. More than once she brought refugees from Shangai, and helped evacuate American diplomats and foreign nationals from that city after the Chinese Communists takeover. In 1961 the *General Gordon* was refitted and, in an economy move, was handed over to the Military Sea Transportation Service and manned by civilians. During the Vietnam war her troop carrying capacity was increased to about 4500 men, plus a 24 man U.S. Navy military department, and a civilian crew of about 300 men.

The officers' accommodation was spartan due to the fact that like all U.S. flag ships, wood was not used in her construction. Decks, bulkheads, bunks, lockers and tables were all built of steel. The troop compartments and mess rooms were air-conditioned but our accommodation was not. This was all right in temperate climes, but under a merciless tropical sun my room became an oven. I shared it with a man called Hank. He was a large, sandy haired man who said little but was not unfriendly.

A few days after my arrival aboard, an announcement was made on the ship's public address system. All hands were to assemble in the ship's main salon (saloon on a British ship), the Captain was aboard and he wanted to talk to the crew. I had never seen this done before and was apt to be scornful of such theatrics. It reminded me of a scene in the wartime movie "In which we serve," when the captain of H.M.S. *Torrens* (Noel Coward) addresses the crew before the ship went into action, and in his best naval fashion begins by saying," Well men...." However I was soon to learn that Captain Robert Landry was not a man to make fun of. He was in his mid-fifties, of sturdy build and commanding manner; the sort of man who was able to maintain discipline and command respect and loyalty from the crew.

Over two hundred men had assembled in the salon when Captain Landry walked in dressed in smart khaki uniform. I was similarly attired but with fewer stripes on my epaulets, and no longer felt ill at ease. He stood on a bench and began by introducing himself. He had been transferred from another ship and needed the co-operation of all of us to make the coming voyage a success. "Whether you are the head of your department or a galley helper, you are important to the ship's team, and if you have a problem I want to hear about it. It is important that we have an efficient and happy ship and I intend to see to it. To all new crew members, welcome aboard."

The Captain and Chief Officer of the 'General Gordon'

It was an impressive performance. In some ships it might have sounded corny but in this ship it worked and I began to sense that Captain Landry was no ordinary man. He now had the crew on his side. The *General Gordon* was a happy ship on an unhappy mission. I thought about other masters I had been with and wondered how many

69

of them could have made life easier for themselves by talking to the crew. American seamen it seemed had more respect for the captain than was the case aboard some British ships I had sailed on.

'General Gordon'. David Johnstone and me. We were the only alien deck officers aboard.

David Johnstone, the other 3rd officer aboard, was a young New Zealander. We became friends, having both been with the Union Steamship Company of New Zealand. He had served his apprenticeship in their ships and I had spent two years in the company's cargo ship 'Waikawa'. He had been enticed to come north to earn higher wages in Canada but had tired of working on ferries, and, having met and married a Canadian girl he needed money to buy a house.

Our orders were to sail to San Diego to embark troops for Vietnam, but the Coast Guard regulations regarding emergency drills had to be carried out first. It was known as a Phase 3; abandon ship and fire fighting exercise. I felt a bit uneasy about this, sensing that we would be subjected to a very thorough testing; and it was. After leaving the dock in Oakland we steamed out into San Francisco Bay and anchored about a mile off Alcatraz Island. Coast Guard inspectors came aboard and with clipboards in hand, ordered a life boat drill.

Earlier I had walked along the boat deck and noted with interest that some of the twenty life boats were nested. A nested boat is one which is stowed within another. This was an arrangement I had never seen before and when I discovered that my station had a nested boat, I felt nervous. But was fortunate in having two experienced seamen with me who knew exactly what to do. So with an air of detached authority I stood back and watched. The drills went without a hitch and I was very relieved when we were awarded a pass mark on the assessment.

But there was more to come. Every officer, from the master down, was given a written test on his knowledge of the International Rules of the Road. A young Coast Guard ensign handed me examination papers and I was instructed to take them to the bridge and fill them out. The questions were multiple choice and some were tricky, but having recently been up for a ticket I had no trouble, however it did bring home to me the fact that aboard American ships nothing was left to chance.

I had come to the United States with certain pre-conceived notions about the sloppy way the Americans ran ships. I was about to learn otherwise. Like all American ships, the licenses of the master and mates of the *General Gordon* were prominently displayed on the bulkhead of the alleyway leading to the bridge. These were framed certificates along with a photograph of the holder. Some men looked very serious, others light-hearted, even jaunty, so it was possible to form an opinion of shipmates before meeting them.

17

Vietnam

After the embarkation of over 4500 troops in San Diego we sailed for Cam Ran Bay, Vietnam. There was tremendous satisfaction in being on the bridge of a large, fast ship en route to the Far East and now I was dressed for the job. I had been outfitted by Penney's Dept. Store in Oakland, who stocked khaki uniforms and regulation style black shoes for the American Merchant Marine.

I was on the 12 to 4 watch with the 2nd mate Jerry Boyd, a skilled navigator, whose motto when working out the ship's position was, measure twice and cut once. "It is easy to make a mistake reading the sextant, measuring a distance on the chart or reading the Nautical Almanac, so I always give it a second glance." said Jerry as he moved the perspex triangles with great dexterity across the chart. I had never seen this done by instruments other than parallel rules, which were apt to slip when not enough downward pressure was used. " Practice makes perfect." said Jerry.

I was impressed by the way he did his job, and we talked about the differences in the American, the British and Canadian daily routine of fixing a ship's position. I told him that as 2nd mate of previous ships it was my job to look after the chronometer. From the very first time I had become a 2nd mate the importance of winding this instrument was paramount, and this had been established firmly in my mind. It was the first thing I thought about when I got out of my bunk at 8am; to forget to wind it was a cardinal sin.

All deep sea ships carried two chronometers, and when the key was inserted in the back seven and a half turns were made to wind the spring to the eight day limit. It would not have mattered if I had not wound it for a day or two, but if the *old man* had noticed this, my job would have been in jeopardy. Having wound the chronometers it was now part of my job to take a forenoon sight. On hearing this Jerry laughed "what the hell for, were you paid overtime?" " Not a cent," I said "that thought never entered my mind. I have been 2nd mate on British, Canadian and New Zealand ships for years. It was the tradition aboard these ships for the 2nd mate to wind the chronometer and take a morning observation. There was a certain mystique about it, a matter of pride in the job. I was used to it." Jerry laughed, " well Tony, that's a load of bull, there's no goddamn mystique about my job. On American ships we get paid extra money for work done off-watch. Of course I take pride in my job too, but I am not here just for the love of it. I expect to be paid for every minute I spend on the bridge. You were doing work on the 3rd mate's watch which he should have done. He had a license and he could have wound the chronometers and taken a sight."

There was no arguing the sense of what Jerry said. "You are right. My God, I am thinking about the thousands of hours of sleep I have lost over the past fifteen years, not to mention the money I should have been paid."

"Never mind, you will not be working for the glory of the job on this ship but you will be paid for any extra time worked. I have already put you on the overtime list for two hours you worked with me on the charts. Uncle Sam can afford it and when the "eagle shits" (American term for pay day) you will be a few bucks ahead, so forget your old ways and you will be better off."

"What method do you use for working out a sight?" said Jerry as he picked up my sextant for inspection, "you won't need this. On American ships, sextants are supplied as part of the navigation equipment."

"That's generous of them" I said with a touch of sarcasm. "I use Marcq St. Hillaire, the intercept method. I take three fore-noon sights, and it takes about 30 minutes to work them out."

"You can halve that by using these H.O. Tables." said Jerry, indicating a set of volumes on a shelf, "you select the one for whatever Latitude we are in. It's much quicker. We will soon convert you to our methods, and that gives you more time to do other things. Which reminds me, the golden rule in the chart room is that nobody comes to the chart table with a cup of godammed coffee in his hand. Last trip, one idiot of a mate spilt a cup all over the chart. The captain nearly hit him and ordered him off the bridge, saying that such carelessness with coffee was grounds for dismissal."

As we made our way across the Pacific I became more accustomed to the American way of doing things. News of my competence must have reached the captain as I was given responsibilities which I had not expected. A life-sized dummy was kept on the upper bridge to be thrown over the side for man overboard drills. These drills were unannounced and I was on watch one afternoon and busy with the weather-fax machine, when I was startled by three long blasts on the ship's whistle. Jerry appeared at the chartroom door, "Tony, there is a man overboard, take over, you have the con." To have control of a ship carrying over 4000 souls suddenly thrust on me was something of a jolt, and for a second I hesitated. Jerry may have noticed this and said " Make a Williamson Turn, the dummy went over the starboard side."

When a man goes overboard the rule is to order the helm to be turned in the same direction as the side he fell over, then a man is sent aloft to spot him in the water. To execute a Williamson Turn the course is altered about 70 degrees; when this is reached, the helm is put hard over in the opposite direction until the ship is on reciprocal of the original course. When, in theory, the man in the water should be directly ahead. The ship was being steered by the iron mike(automatic steering device) and when in this mode, the quartermaster's duty was to stand and watch the compass. I ordered him to engage the manual steering and apply 20 degrees of right rudder. I had to overcome the inclination to use the word starboard as on American ships alterations of course are ordered as left or right rudder. At first I thought this a rather unseamanlike way of giving orders but then realized that there was a good reason for it. The use of the word port on the bridge at sea could be misconstrued by the helmsman with disastrous results. The words port and starboard were only used aboard American ships in reference to the side of the ship, the port lifeboats, for example or the starboard gangway.

I had put the engines on "Stand by" wondering whether I should slow the ship down, as we were making 20 knots, when the captain arrived on the bridge. To my surprise he didn't say a word, merely picking up a pair of binoculars to scan the waters for the dummy. Meanwhile the emergency boat's crew had gone to their station and were preparing to lower the boat. Now I had to manoeuvre the ship, something I had never done before. Indeed if I had moved the engine telegraph when I was a lowly 3rd mate aboard a British ship at sea, it would surely have caused the master to come bounding onto the bridge.

I remember the commotion aboard my first ship the *Burma* when a first trip apprentice was told to polish the brass telegraph. The handle was at "Full Ahead" and when he needed to polish behind it he moved the handle to "Stop." There must have been considerable excitement down in the engine room, but even more for the master who was in his bunk. He tumbled out in a frightful hurry thinking that the ship was " In extremis." The poor, ignorant apprentice wished he was elsewhere and had chosen another career, after all the imprecations from the captain had fallen about his head.

When the Williamson Turn had been completed I reduced speed to slow and soon after the lookout shouted that the dummy was in sight, fine on the port bow less than a mile away. The engines were stopped and by the time I had taken the way off the ship and made a lee for the rescue boat, the dummy was only a ship's length away. Fortunately the weather was fairly calm and it was retrieved in short order. My performance was considered adequate and I felt pleased with myself. Little did I realize that before long I would be involved in a real rescue at sea.

We had two quartermasters on our watch. Both were black men and a study in contrasts. Mitchell was a taciturn, bad-tempered man who seemed intent on making everyone as miserable as he was. From the very first I was aware of the likelihood of racial tensions aboard. There had been rioting in Los Angeles and I was determined to avoid getting into any potentially explosive situation, which wasn't easy when giving an order to Mitchell, because he had a way of challenging it. He knew the ship and the routine better than I did and was apt to ignore an order. I chose to let it pass when this happened, rather than make an issue of it and find that I was in the wrong, but I knew that sooner or later I had to make a stand if a situation arose when the safety of the ship was at risk. Sure enough it came sooner than I expected.

The captain's standing orders stated than when another ship came within three miles of us the steering was to be changed from automatic to manual steering. I was in charge of the watch while Jerry was busy in the chartroom, when an approaching ship was now 3 miles away. I told Mitchell to disengage the iron mike and take the wheel. "No need to" was his reply, " we are well clear." Sensing trouble I was determined not to give way and said, "that's not the point, I am ordering you to take the wheel." Mitchell hesitated and I thought that he would refuse to obey, but Jerry appeared in the doorway and Mitchell, muttering something under his breath, took the wheel.

It was difficult to strike a balance between exercising what authority I had and maintaining good relations within the watch. No such problem existed with the other quartermaster. Willy was the most affable of men. He made my job easy when he would politely tell me the answer to whatever it was I was unsure of and go about his duty without any fuss.

One of the best seaman aboard was John Hegler, a man in his sixties. John was a granite faced, broad shouldered man of medium height who knew his job. It soon became evident that he was used to hard work and was the sort of man who knew what to do without being told. When the ship was in port the mate told me to check the lifeboats and, as we had ten of them it was a big job, but it was made easier when John was sent to help me. It was a pleasure to work with him and although somewhat taciturn by nature I was able to draw him out. As we worked he told me about some of the adventures he had during his thirty years at sea. He had grown up in Colorado but as a boy had always wanted to go to sea, so left home at 16 and went to San Francisco. There he found a job as a seaman on a small coaster running to ports in Alaska.

On American ships the officer on watch could not use his own words when making entries into the log book. This removed the possibility of using the colourful prose sometimes found in log books where the mate was free to describe events as he saw them. A set terminology was laid down by the U.S.Coast Guard. When a ship put to sea the log book was written up showing the number of officers, crew, passengers if any, and the amount of stores and fuel aboard. This was followed by "this ship being in all respects ready for sea, manned and equipped according to the United States Coast Guard regulations." At the end of each watch the rough log had to be re-written into the fair copy.

A four hour bridge watch aboard the *General Gordon* was hard work. Indeed I seldom had time to pause for a cup of coffee, which was always readily available on American ships. Keeping track of the ship's position, by use of the loran if the skies were overcast, attending to weather maps, and constantly filling in the log with the minutest details. When I was sent on an inspection tour of the ship it was a welcome diversion. Each day I would vary my route through the maze of alleyways into a different troop deck. There was an efficient system of identifying one's location throughout the ship. I had only to look up to see numbers placed at various intervals on the bulkheads. The sign 1-4-148 meant the starboard side of the 4th deck at frame 148. As I carried a sound-powered phone, I only had to plug it into the numerous jacks at hand and report my location to the damage control room abaft the bridge.

The main purpose of my tour was to inspect the ship's brig. It was located at the forward end of the lowest troop deck and there was room for fifteen prisoners. A white helmeted military guard stood outside the cells. I was tempted to enquire about the prisoners and the reasons for their being in the brig, but the men of the Military Police were stony-faced, and not given to idle chatter.

When I arrived the guard stood stiffly to attention and without a flicker of emotion reported the number of prisoners adding "All in order, Sir," I returned to the bridge and entered this into the log book. Time in the brig was punishment for such infractions as gambling, smoking in the troop decks, disorderly behavior, disrespect for an officer, and oddly, for hanging clothing over ships' piping. There were usually about ten men in the brig and they seemed to spend most of their time sleeping.

It was a novel experience to be at sea with so many passengers aboard. Among the ship's complement was a military department whose job it was to maintain discipline and to make sure that the troops were exercised, fed and ready for whatever lay ahead. They acted as liaison between the military and the ship's officers. Three doctors headed a medical department. A well equipped hospital with an operation theatre ensured the very best of care for all aboard.

Feeding so many men was a big challenge for the cooks. I visited the baker's department and watched in awe as large trays of dough were pushed into the ovens with long poles. "How many loaves do you bake in a day?" I asked. "Over 700 and almost as many pies, these guys get nothing but the best," was the reply.

After sunset the movies began. Three shows were shown simultaneously throughout the ship; two in spacious mess rooms and one out on the open after deck. So as the ship steamed east under a starry sky, and rolling easily in gentle swells, cat calls, whistles and shouts arose from the decks, as hundreds of GI's watched the flickering screen which had been put up near the mainmast. They sat astride the derricks, squatted on the deck and a few hung in the rigging, all to view the latest Hollywood epic. The appearance of scantily clad girls provoked the loudest shouts of approval. In the officers' mess a fourth movie was shown. It wasn't always worth watching but it was a refuge from the stifling heat of our accommodation.

There were over 4500 soldiers aboard and they were remarkably well behaved when one considers that they were conscripted to fight in an unpopular war from which many would not return. Most of them were fresh faced kids in their late teens who had never left the shores of the U.S.A. I spoke to one man who quite openly expressed his fear of what lay ahead. He came from Kentucky and he wondered how his Pa could run the farm without him.

After a passage of thirteen days the coast of Vietnam came in sight and after picking up the American Navy pilot we entered the harbour of Cam Ranh Bay. It had been developed into a large port by the U.S. Military to handle a vast amount of war equipment. We tied up alongside a modern wharf, gangways were put ashore and the troops carrying their M16 rifles went ashore and into a line of trucks. There was the sound of gunfire in the distance and helicopters whirled over us and headed towards the hills. The Tet Offensive had begun, and heavy fighting was going on in the jungle surrounding the hills in the distance. We heard that some of the trucks carrying the soldiers came under enemy fire within minutes of leaving the dockside.

A day later we were at sea bound for Nha Trang. It was during the middle watch at night and, as we were in the war zone, no navigation lights were shown. It was an occasion when I learnt a lesson in self-confidence. We were ten miles off a low lying coast steaming at 20 knots, and the only way to fix our position was by radar bearings. It was a nerve-wracking business as I tried to compare the chart with what I saw on the radar screen. At our high speed it was essential to fix the position every 20 minutes and I was very busy moving from the radar to the chartroom table and, under a dim orange light, laying the bearings onto the chart. To my surprise the fix showed that we were making 25 knots. I thought that I had made a mistake and was inclined to ignore it but took more bearings, which confirmed the fact that were indeed where the fixes put us, and making high speed. It was a good thing that I believed this as we arrived at our destination earlier than expected due to a strong current pushing us.

The beach at Cam Ranh Bay.

18

Man Overboard

It was my second trip from San Francisco to Vietnam. I was now on the 8- 2 watch with Ed Daly who I soon discovered was very difficult to get along with. He was a graduate of Kings Point Merchant Marine Academy in Maryland, U.S.A. He had been at sea during the war years but had left soon after. A twenty year absence from the sea meant that he had lost touch with certain aspects of navigation. He was probably aware of this lack and consequently was extremely sensitive about what he perceived as any challenge to his authority. This caused high tension on the bridge in contrast to being on watch with the 2nd officer Jerry Boyd.

I became aware of Ed's shortcomings during our first watch together. We had dropped the San Francisco pilot off and we were heading out towards the Farralones Rocks and into the open waters of the Pacific. There were a few ships ahead and Ed picked up the binoculars to look at a tanker on our starboard bow. She was about 7 miles off and heading away from our course thus there was no danger of collision. To my astonishment Ed announced his intention to alter course.

Seamen can usually discern the direction of a ship by her profile and everyone on the bridge, except the officer in charge, could plainly see that this vessel was heading north. I hesitated to interfere but as he seemed intent on giving the order I said "There is no need to alter course, she is clearing us." With an expression of disbelief and anger, Ed seemed about to explode but thought better of it on seeing that the tanker had moved clear. This unhappy exchange worried me. There were now bad feelings between us and I realized that as the junior officer of the watch I was in an awkward position. I wondered what I would do if a serious situation developed and the ship was put in danger. I was to find out later.

Our course took us to the north of the Hawaiian Islands and after three days at sea we were 400 miles off these islands, steaming at 19 knots in a rough sea and heavy swell. The weather was fine and warm and this had brought the troops out on the decks. For most of them it was probably their first trip to sea, and whatever thoughts they may have had about what lay ahead, at the moment, it must have seemed a pleasant change from an army camp ashore. As they staggered about trying to keep their footing on unfamiliar, heaving decks, the ship was rolling considerably, there were shouts, cat-calls and the usual boisterous behavior. This did not prevent me from taking an afternoon nap, which was one of the advantages of being on the morning watch, when, half-awake, I heard the shout "Man overboard."

I was inclined at first to ignore it. It was usually shouted in thoughtless jest but this time I sensed a certain urgency. I jumped to my feet, dressed and rushed out on deck. I met the chief officer Mr Hottle. He handed me a lifejacket and a walkie-talkie. " A man has gone overboard. Take the port emergency boat away and keep in touch with the bridge."

Hardly able to contain my excitement I made my way to the boat past a crowd of soldiers. An officer arrived and ordered them to clear away from the area. When I reached the boat four seamen, an engineer, the military doctor and an assistant medic were already aboard, I scrambled in and we were lowered down. Launching a boat in a rough sea is usually a tricky business, fending her off the side of the ship and releasing the falls at the right time calls for good judgement, however we got clear without damage. I ordered full ahead on the motor and steered towards a wisp of smoke (a smoke float had been thrown over with a life ring) about half a mile away.

Once clear of the ship's bow we felt the full force of rough seas and a heavy swell, and soon we were swept by a succession of sprays and some solid water over the bow. This forced me to reduce speed. All aboard were soaked, not that it mattered in warm weather but a heavy swell when viewed from a lifeboat is a daunting sight, as we were swept up the side of a steep wall of water. When we reached the life-ring and began scouring the water for the missing man, I glanced astern, the masts of the 20,000 ton *General Gordon* was all that was visible, the rest of her was hidden behind a big swell.

After an hour searching in vain I received the order to return to the ship. Even in the lee of the ship there was a considerable swell, and on reaching the falls great care was required to hook them on and take out the turns, before we were lifted up. Only a seaman can appreciate the difficulty of launching or retrieving a boat in a rough sea; one moment the boat was lifted almost to deck level and the next we would drop ten feet. The mate on deck ordered the winch to take the weight at exactly the right time, and when he did there was a terrific jerk as the 4 ton load seemed sufficient to tear the davits out of the deck. Soon we were back aboard.

I reached the bridge as the Chaplain had finished reading a prayer for the lost G.I. who was from Puerto Rico. He was only 19 years old. An inquiry into this tragedy was held during which witnesses said that the G.I. was standing on the fantail (aftermost section of the ship) with a crowd of men when he suddenly climbed onto the rail and dived overboard. He came to the surface briefly in the ships wake and then disappeared. The alarm was sounded and life rings thrown over. We had done our utmost to find him. All to no avail.

The stars and stripes were lowered to half mast, the telegraph was put on full speed and we resumed the voyage. Captain Landry met me in the chartroom, " On American ships you are entitled to a drink on these occasions, it is for medicinal purposes. What would you like, rum or whiskey?" I was taken aback, but not about to refuse. "Thank you, Captain," I replied. "Rum please." It went down very well.

Aboard American ships the regulations about drinking alcohol and taking drugs were rigorously enforced. I accompanied officers on inspection tours of the crew's quarters to search for evidence. These searches were unannounced and presumably unexpected, but although it was common knowledge that marijuana was being smoked, no one was caught during the time I was aboard. One of the radio officers was not so fortunate; he was reported drunk on duty, his room was searched and several bottles of scotch whisky were found. I then witnessed an unusual ceremony.

Captain Landry and other senior officers gathered on the wing of the bridge, the radio man was summoned. He appeared in a rumpled khaki uniform looking thoroughly dejected, his eyes downcast and bleary. It could have been a scene outside a seedy dockside tavern instead of the bridge of a ship at sea. The captain began to read the charges against him; he picked up one of the bottles, removed the cap and emptied the contents overboard. It would have made a connoisseur of good whisky weep. The wretched radio officer was confined to his quarters to sober up.

19

The China Sea

Our route took us into the South China Sea via the Philippines. The perfectly shaped cone of Mount Mayan rose above the horizon marking the entrance to the Straits of San Bernardino. For many aboard, this was their first sight of Asia. For the next ten hours we threaded our way past hundreds of beautiful islands. When I came on watch at 8 p.m. the land was far astern. We were now in the war zone and steaming at 20 knots without showing navigation lights, which was the cause of some anxiety when meeting other ships. There was still tension on the bridge because of strained relations between Ed Daly and me. There was no chitchat between us; we only spoke when it was absolutely necessary to do so. With two radar sets it was important to monitor the screens frequently as we steamed in total darkness.

Shortly before midnight an echo appeared on the radar screens. It was on our starboard bow about 6 miles away. I placed the cursor on the echo to determine whether the bearing was changing, it was not, and it became apparent that the ship was closing at high speed. Unless we altered course a collision was likely. Picking up the binoculars I peered into the darkness but nothing was visible. Wondering whether the officer in charge was aware of the approaching ship I said, " Ed, the ship on our starboard bow is 5 miles away, the bearing is steady, she is closing fast." I cannot remember his exact reply or whether he said anything, but what I do recall is the acute anxiety I felt as I waited for him to take action. He remained silent as I continued to report the decreasing range. I wondered how long I should wait before ordering an alteration of course.

When the echo had reached the 2 mile ring I could wait no longer and shouted to the helmsman " 15 degrees right rudder." The ship swung quickly to starboard and none too soon, as moments later the dark shape of a destroyer appeared less than a mile ahead of us; the foam at her bow evidence that she was steaming at high speed. She swept past our port side and disappeared into the night. After we had returned to our course there was some muttering and angry words from Ed. I drew a breath of relief but said nothing, it was an unpleasant moment when silence seemed the wisest course. I felt uneasy about what lay ahead but confident that I had done the right thing.

After being relieved at midnight, I was on my way below when I met the captain. His usual placid manner was now one of concern. "Mr. Winstanley, I want to speak to you." He ushered me into his room and sat at his desk. "I saw what happened a few minutes ago. From now on I want you to take charge of the watch." I felt relief that I had not received a reprimand. News of my action must have reached him. "Yes Captain, but this places me in a difficult position with Mr. Daly." Captain Landry smiled wryly, "Yes, I am aware of that, but the ship's safety comes first. Mr. Daly has a problem. If you have any difficulty come and see me."

Oddly enough, from that moment on there was peace on the 8-12 watch. The captain had evidently spoken to Ed Daly and with considerable skill had managed to soothe ruffled feelings. I was surprised to find that Ed became quite friendly towards me, even though I was now in charge of the watch. Weeks later when we met in a servicemen's club in Sasebo, Japan, he called me to his table and insisted that I have a drink with him. A remarkable turn around of attitude, and I could only admire a man who had the character to accept an outsider taking over his job.

20

The War Zone

We anchored 3 miles off the beach at Danang surrounded by many other ships loaded with war materials; among these were several wartime built Liberty ships which had proved their endurance, despite early doubts about all welded ships. Landing craft came alongside and the troops began to disembark. They soon became aware that a war was in progress, as the sound of gunfire came from the densely wooded hills adjacent to the military base at Danang.

Several helicopter gunships flew past like giant eagles on the hunt for the elusive Viet Cong, who had recently made daring raids on the base. There was no way of telling the difference between them and any other Vietnamese. We had been warned of sabotage, particularly when the shore workers came aboard to unload cargo, and there was no way of distinguishing between friend or foe. Earlier the troopship *Geiger* had anchored here and when discharging cargo, someone noticed a suspicious bundle lying under a pile of life-floats on the fore deck. The bomb squad was called and defused a device (12 lbs. of T.N.T.), powerful enough to have blown a large hole in the side of the ship.

Soon after our arrival, I was standing on the fo'c's'le head and witnessed an incident which brought home an unpleasant aspect of the war. There were many sampans fishing in the waters around us and all of them flew the striped yellow and black flag of South Vietnam. No doubt this was to show that ostensibly they were loyal South Vietnamese, although there were strong suspicion that some were Viet Cong sympathizers.

A U.S. Navy patrol boat came alongside a sampan, which was lying only a few feet from our side. The fisherman had his wife and children aboard. A burly navy seaman jumped aboard, grabbed the fisherman by the hair and began beating him on the head with a stick. I could hear the thumps as the blows rained down on him. There were screams of protest, as it was evident that he had been unable to show any means of identification. There was shouting and wailing from the women as the fisherman was dragged aboard the launch and taken away. I looked away in disgust at the brutality of this attack and wondered what would happen to the fisherman.

We heard reports of divers attacking ships at anchor. Wearing breathing apparatus these men would swim under water and attach mines to the hulls of ships. One of these divers had been caught after he surfaced near a ship he had attacked. The mine went off prematurely and he was barely alive as blood oozed out of his mouth and ears.

Although we were in a war zone, shore leave was permitted, unless an attack by North Vietnamese forces or the Viet Cong occurred and a red alert was in effect. After three weeks aboard ship most of the crew were anxious to see what life in a war torn city looked like, and I was no exception. I had been in Saigon in 1938, when it was the capital of French Indo China, and I was curious to see Danang. Before the liberty launch arrived I went to the pursers office to draw some money. The currency regulations were strict, U.S. dollars were not to be taken ashore. I was given M.P.C. notes, (Military Payment Certificates) in lieu of dollars, and these had to be taken to an exchange office ashore where they were exchanged for Vietnamese piastres, which were almost worthless. With a pocketful of crumpled, grubby notes I went in search of a cool drink, and walked up a crowded street lined with ramshackle shops.

It was exhilarating to be back in the Orient once again. Even though this was a country torn apart by war, there were the same colourful, energetic people I had seen in 1938. The girls neatly attired in their chung-sun skirts, many of them riding bicycles, with poise and dignity. The rickshaws of colonial days had disappeared; a man running between the shafts of this vehicle was considered as degrading and it had been replaced by a pedi-cab. The passenger sat behind the pedaler in a pedi-cab. A swifter but noisier conveyance was a three-wheeled motor bike which emitted a cloud of smoke from its spluttering exhaust.

It was mid -afternoon, the heat was intense and I needed a cool drink. The O.K. Bar seemed a likely place to find one. A group of American soldiers stood languidly outside drinking beer with their heavily made-up Vietnamese pick-ups. Pushing through the crowded room I reached the bar and ordered a drink. On receiving a foaming glass of San Miguel beer, I took a handful of piastres from my pocket. The Vietnamese bar keeper became excited and pushed my proffered local currency away, "You have American dollar, No?" When I replied that I didn't, he became agitated, especially after seeing that I had already taken a gulp of beer to quench my thirst.

I strayed innocently into an area of Danang frequented by Viet-Cong

Events might have taken an ugly turn if an American sailor hadn't intervened, with the generous offer to pay for my drink with a U.S. greenback. I was pleased to accept this and thanked him. He ordered a beer and we sat down. His name was Hank, a bosun's mate aboard a tank landing craft; he came from Chicago and was counting the days until he could return home. "I have been in this god-dammed place for too long, it's a year since I left the States. Four more weeks and I'm out of here." He looked at my handful of piastres, " You may as well give them away. It is a military offence to use Yankee dollars, here but no one wants worthless piasters, and these people won't take them, so how the hell can we buy a drink? With Yankee dollars that's how." Hank talked about his ship; " We take supplies to wherever they are needed around the coast. Sometimes we run into trouble when the V.C. fire at us from the jungle, but our guys let them have it with cannon fire."

"The worst time is when we are running up the Saigon river. Some guys were killed on another landing craft when they were hit by fire from the Cong. They were hiding in the trees on the river bank less than 300 feet away. They are full of tricks the bastards, they even use kids to attack us. A few weeks ago one of our ships was on the way up river and was blown up by a mine. Moments before it exploded, the lookout on the bridge spotted two kids standing at the waters edge and waved to them. What he didn't see was that one of the little girls held a trip wire in her hand which she pulled at the precise moment. The mine blew our bow off. A raid was made on the village near where this happened but of course nobody knew anything about it."

"I'm glad I'm not in the godammed infantry. They have a helluva life out there in the jungle, counting the days to the end of tour of duty. Some guys get hit hours before they are due to be shipped back State-Side. I have heard of men who hate it so bad in Nam, that they injure themselves on purpose to get on the sick list. They go out on patrol looking for gooks they cannot find, and maybe a couple of guys get killed. Things look bad and morale is low, they smoke a few joints and when the officer orders them to go on another patrol, there's a fragging. Do you know what a fragging is?"

I told him that I had never heard of the word. Hank ordered another beer and lit a cigarette, "The men refuse to obey the order and when the officer repeats it, a guy shouts "Fuck off!" and shoots him dead. That's the end of it and no questions asked. That's fragging." I asked Hank whether he had taken any R&R (Rest and Recreation) since he came to Vietnam. "Yeah, I went to one near Vung Tau after I had been over here 6 months. It was o.k. for a while but I got tired of it. I should have taken my R & R in Hawaii, or in Bangkok where the action is."

The aroma of cooking wafted in from the street where the owner of a food cart was basting chickens on a spit, and it reminded me that it was time to go back aboard and have supper. It was dark by the time I reached the jetty, where a crowd of seamen waited for the launch to take them back to their ships. Among the crowd were white helmeted Military Police,(called snow drops), whose job was to check the identity of people landing and departing. When the launch arrived I moved with the crowd to go aboard and was suddenly seized by near panic when I realized that I did not have my identity card with me. To make matters worse, a red alert had been sounded and I knew what can happen to anyone caught ashore without papers.

I boarded the launch without being challenged but my troubles were not over. I became exceedingly anxious as the M.P. came closer, pushing his way through the crowd inspecting identity cards. I saw a possible way out of the dilemma, and at great cost to my nervous system succeeded, by concealing myself in a doorway. Sweating profusely I tried to appear as inconspicuous as possible. By pure good fortune I eluded the M.P.'s scrutiny, and after an agonizingly long launch trip we finally reached the ship. I darted up the gangway feeling like an escapee from a chain gang.

'General Gordon' at anchor
off Nha Trang.

But the excitements of the day were not over. Shortly after midnight I was on my way to my cabin when a loud explosion shook the ship. I ran out on deck and saw a mass of flames and billowing smoke on the land a few miles away from us. "They have hit the army base", said the mate who had just got out of his bunk, " Call the crew out on deck, we could be next." I returned to the bridge where the 2nd mate had already rung the alarm. There was nothing further to do except wait for the 'all clear', which came two hours later. News reached us that the base had been attacked by mortar fire from the Viet Cong. Several planes had been destroyed, a gasoline tank had gone up and thirty men were killed. It seems that four men could mount a mortar attack; one man carried the barrel, another the tripod and the other two, the bombs. The damage inflicted was considerable.

After this we weighed anchor and sailed south for Nha Trang. There were the sounds of warfare there too. Our entry into this picturesque harbour was delayed because of heavy fighting in the area, and we lay off the coast for the night, steaming at slow speed. As darkness descended over Nha Trang star shells lit up the hills, and we could hear the staccato rattle of gunfire as helicopter gunships strafed the thickly wooded hills, outside the city. At dawn the fighting stopped and Nha Trang, shimmering in the heat, appeared to be as tranquil and prosperous as a town on the French Riviera.

Nha Trang
I asked the launch operator to take me to the tanker in
the background. The house on the hill owned by the
Dragon Lady.

We entered the harbour and anchored not far from a headland, on which a large white villa stood. It was owned by the notorious Dragon Lady, Madame Nhu, wife of the puppet president of Vietnam. I was able to persuade the Vietnamese operator of a launch to take me out in the harbour, as I wanted to take photographs of the *General Gordon* and the villa on the hill. According to the Stars and Stripes (the U.S. Army newspaper), Madame Nhu and her daughter spent most of their time in Paris buying clothes, jewelry, and other extravagances, thus depleting the hard-pressed South Vietnamese treasury in the process. This item of news must have made many G.I.s wonder why they were in Vietnam.

21

Sasebo

On my third trip to Vietnam we sailed from San Francisco to Hawaii to pick up special troops who had been doing jungle warfare training on the islands. It was my first visit to Honolulu and as we came alongside the wharf, a military band struck up a rousing march to give the embarking soldiers a good send-off. I was invited to dinner by a commander in the U.S. Navy, and his wife. He had been the Naval Attaché at the Canadian base in Esquimalt, B.C. His daughter had attended the same school as my daughter Jennifer, and they became friends. I was taken on a tour of the base at Pearl Harbour and saw the memorial to the battleship Arizona.

A few days after leaving Hawaii we heard the news that the *General Gordon* would not return to the States, but run on a shuttle service between Pusan, Korea and ports in Vietnam. Our logistic port was to be Sasebo, in Japan. The U.S. government had persuaded the South Korean Government to supply soldiers to fight in Vietnam. They were known as R.O.K. (Republic of Korea) troops whose tour of 13 months duty in Vietnam, was the same as the time spent overseas by the American G.I.'s. The Koreans were only too willing to get into the fray, especially as they would receive the same pay as the Americans.

We arrived in Sasebo a few days before Christmas 1967. There was snow on the hills in the background of this naval base on Kyusho Island. Japan had changed dramatically since I had visited Kure aboard the *Samdaring* in 1946. It was now a dynamic, industrious nation, building giant ships. I walked into a shipyard close to where we were docked and saw a very large tanker nearing completion. Ships of this size were built in a dry dock and floated out on completion. I looked at this 200,000 tonner and was amazed by her vast bulk. The plating at her fore end was covered by web-like bamboo scaffolding held together by rope lashings. This seemed like a primitive and flimsy structure, an anachronism, in contrast to the tubular steel scaffolding used in western shipyards. I received permission to board this huge ship, and walked up a gangway which was built in two stages, because her main deck was so high a single gangway would have been at too steep an angle to reach it. Standing on the bridge, I looked at the fo'c's'le head nearly a 1000 feet away, and thought about the first tanker I had served on. The Murena was a mere 450 feet long and she had a crew of about fifty men, whereas this automated giant would be manned by half that many.

During our stay in Sasebo one seaman was knocked down by a taxi. He wasn't badly hurt and after treatment in hospital he returned aboard. The taxicab company was very concerned about his welfare and the owner came aboard. A group of us gathered in the Captain's room to watch, as the owner offered gifts to the injured man, and a letter of concern was read by the mate. It was an example of good relations at a time when there were tensions, because of the presence of U.S. forces in Japan.

I shared my room with another mate, Bud Fenton. He was of medium height, fat and fussy about body odour, so much so that he doused himself with copious quantities of highly perfumed lotions. It was important to him to smell right and the stench of exotic perfumes traveled with Bud wherever he went. It seemed strange aboard a ship yet there was nothing effeminate about Bud, he just had an obsession about scent.

Sometimes he kept me awake when I happened to be trying to sleep, for he was constantly twiddling the tuning button of his radio. But he was affable enough, and when he wasn't listening to rubbish on the radio, he delighted in recounting his numerous adventures ashore in search of feminine company. He would go into lurid detail, and I tired of hearing these oft repeated yarns. Bud had talent of another kind I had never seen in a ship's officer; he was a licensed compass adjuster, and had exercised his expertise on our compasses before we left San Francisco. However his main preoccupation was self-indulgence.

I had been ashore in Sasebo, and after an evening wandering the crowded streets in pouring rain, I was glad to back aboard. I hadn't been asleep an hour when the door opened, the light turned on, and there was Bud acting as if he had been savaged by a pack of wild dogs.

He sat down heavily and groaned. He had had a bad night and was anxious to give me the details.

If a man was looking for excitement and fun in Sasebo the place to go was Saki Town. There were dance halls, taverns and places where one could gamble, but Bud needed a massage. When he entered a parlour his mind was on other things besides a good rub. After paying a hefty admission fee he expected to be attended to by a bevy of gorgeous masseuses, indeed the neon sign hanging over the entrance promised as much. Bud was handed a ticket and directed to a door along a passage and, with mounting excitement he entered a room, was told to remove his clothes, and wait.

Having disrobed, he stood, all 220lbs of flabby expectation. Suddenly a curtain parted, two hefty women of uncertain age dressed in white blouses and baggy pants, grabbed Bud, threw him to the floor face down, and before he could get up, jumped on his recumbent form and began kneading his ample back with their feet, just as a baker would knead a lump of dough. All resistance was futile. Bud tried to stand up and protest that he hadn't paid for this unwarranted assault on his person, but to no avail, his assailants attacked with renewed vigour. He was flattened again, pummeled mercilessly and by the time they had finished he felt as if he had been trampled by an angry elephant. Bruised, battered and much the wiser he retrieved his clothing, slunk out, hailed a taxi and was relieved to reach the safety of the ship. After hearing this gripping tale, I was now wide awake and inclined to laugh, but I managed to feel some sympathy for him so kept a straight face. Bud, on the other hand was angry at having been rubbed the wrong way. He was not inclined to return to Saki Town.

22

Pusan, and R.O.K. Bottom

We sailed north to Pusan, in South Korea, to take on R.O.K. troops for ports in Vietnam. There was some delay in embarking the soldiers and we lay alongside the dock for two days. It was an opportunity for the mate to get some much needed maintenance work done, and cheap shore labour was ordered to chip the outside steel decks. A gang of about thirty labourers came aboard and set to work with a vengeance. The deafening clatter of hammers hitting the decks could be heard throughout the ship. The workers were a tough looking bunch of middle-aged women dressed in shapeless baggy clothing, who squatted down on their haunches as they laboured amid the dust. To escape this racket, I went ashore past a steely-eyed Korean military guard who scrutinized my pass and reminded me of what I had heard earlier; that the Koreans were a very tough people indeed, accustomed to hardship, and it was wise not to aggravate them by failing to respect their customs.

The city of Pusan appeared drab and grey in comparison to Sasebo. Whereas the new Japan had achieved prosperity, Korea had not yet recovered from the 1952 war. The streets teemed with people going about their business, yet there were signs of poverty and desperation among a populace trying to scrape a living. I watched in fascination as a man rode past making the best use of a bike I had ever seen; a steel frame had been welded to carry loads above the rider. On this, a pile of wood was balanced three feet above him. Decrepit buses belching clouds of smoke and crammed with passengers, jostled for right of way in a manner I had not seen since my visits to pre-war India.

Troop trains appeared on the quayside and I watched as several hundred R.O.K. soldiers lined up waiting to embark. They were a rag-tag lot, compared to American soldiers, wearing rough, shapeless dark green uniforms. They were men from the impoverished mountain regions of South Korea who, it seems, had never seen the sea before.

They were unable to comprehend that the ship that they were now about to board, was afloat, and not part of the land.

We sailed with about 5500 troops bound for Camn Ranh Bay, Vietnam. A contingent of voyage control officers was aboard to maintain strict discipline, and this was enforced in a manner different from the U.S. army. When carrying G.I.'s there were always a few men in the ship's brig. It was empty when Korean soldiers were aboard. Whenever a soldier broke the rules he was dealt with immediately by the Korean Voyage Control Officers. It became a common sight to witness these officers wading in with sticks, fists and boots to break up a fight and restore order. It seemed rather a brutal way of policing but it was effective. I was standing on the boat deck talking to Ensign George Gratz one afternoon, shortly after we sailed, when our attention was drawn to a group of soldiers who were shouting at each other. Fists were flying and blood was flowing as one soldier was hit on the nose.

But the Control officers were on the scene very quickly. They tore into the combatants, hitting out with their short, heavy batons and knocking three men down. That apparently wasn't enough, as they followed the assault with well-aimed kicks on the backs and backsides of the recumbent men. It was a sorry spectacle and I was unable to resist saying, "Any Control officer who kicks a Korean soldier in the arse, has struck R.O.K. bottom." Ensign Gratz pondered that remark and groaned.

The voyage Control officers had other duties too; instructing the soldiers in the use of western style toilets. This took some time with so many men aboard, so, for the first few days at sea a walk about the troop decks at night was precarious, as men relieved themselves haphazardly in random places, as they would in the mountains. With over 4500 Korean troops aboard, the catering department had to supply a diet consisting mainly of rice, beans, pork and the favourite Korean pickled cabbage known as Kimchi. This gave off a powerful aroma which pervaded the entire ship.

On reaching Camn Ranh Bay the smartly dressed U.S. Naval boarding officer, Lieutenant Rowntree was one of the first up the gangway. On reaching the bridge he spoke to Captain Landry, "I have been in the military for fifteen years and seen how the army deals with men who cut loose and break the law, but these Koreans don't mess about. They shot a man a few days ago, right there behind the freight sheds." The lieutenant sipped his black coffee. " A Vietnamese woman reported that she had been raped by a R.O.K soldier. Their commander ordered an inquiry but nobody was talking, so a platoon of men was lined up. The girl in question was told to identify her assailant, this she did; he was taken behind the shed and shot. Whether he was guilty or not was irrelevant. He may have been the wrong man but I guess there will be no more rapes around here for awhile. Korean soldiers are a hard lot." In battle they gave no quarter and expected none. Reports of their treatment of prisoners caused concern to the U.S. Military; when stories filtered out that Korean soldiers were shooting prisoners, a fate they evidently expected themselves when captured.

Within a few hours of disembarking the troops were on their way to

Pusan, S. Korea. Ed Daly and me on deck to watch the troops embark. The officer on left had been using his stick to keep order.

the battlefront, and another load of battle weary soldiers who had completed their tour of duty in Vietnam, came aboard. We expected to sail immediately but there was cargo to take aboard and to load it we anchored in the bay. Several barges were towed from the shore and they came alongside. These barges were loaded with hundreds of wooden boxes piled three high, and each about 6ft x 6ft in size.

The Korean soldiers had accumulated a lot of merchandise, during their spells away from the fighting, and needed boxes to carry the loot back home. They would head for the P.X. store to stock-up on such items as radios, tape recorders, and television sets. Some boxes were very heavy, being full of such delicacies as canned fruit, a luxury unknown in Korea. When the loading began trouble erupted down in the cargo hold. The work was done by Vietnamese stevedores and they were watched closely by Korean soldiers, concerned about the careful handling of their precious boxes. They would lean over the hatch coaming and shout threats at the men working below if they thought a box was being roughly handled. I was on duty and down in the hold when two Korean soldiers began beating up two of the workers.

The Vietnamese people are small in stature, whereas the average Korean is taller and stronger, and in this instance the stevedores put up little resistance and were knocked down and kicked. I rushed up on deck in search of the control officers, who arrived on the scene with their batons, and order was quickly restored. The stevedores then refused to work and demanded protection. This was supplied, and work resumed.

Our arrival back in Pusan was an unforgettable event. As we approached the jetty the sound of brass bands and cheering from a vast throng echoed across the harbour. Flags and banners waved in the breeze. A contingent of girls in brightly coloured costumes began to sing as we drew alongside the jetty. It was a hot summer's day and it appeared that a large portion of the city's population had assembled to welcome the returning warriors. Before dusk the ship was cleared of troops, a gang of workers had been aboard to clean the troop decks, and another contingent of 4500 soldiers came aboard. Once more we sailed back to Vietnam.

The hottest place on the coast seemed to be Qui Nhon. The steel decks on the ship were hot enough to blister bare feet, and our accommodation was stifling. The mountains in the distance shimmered in the heat and the notion of going ashore was not appealing. Instead I decided to go aboard a British Shell tanker anchored nearby. The liberty boat dropped me off at her accommodation ladder and I was soon gulping down a cold beer in the 3rd mate's comfortable, air-conditioned room.

Tom Thornton had served his time in tankers and stayed with the Shell Oil Company because the pay and conditions were better than in cargo ships. The ship had been away from her home port for eight months. "We get danger money on this coast and we earn it too. A few months ago we were attacked as we went up the Saigon River. A Viet Cong opened fire at us from the bank of the river and the Chinese quartermaster at the wheel was killed. We nearly ran ashore. It was horrible; blood all over the wheelhouse. Now we carry armed guards when we go to Saigon. It's a dicey business and I will be glad to get home. By the time we get back to the U.K. I will have enough sea time , and money, to go up for my mate's ticket."

A contingent of troops had been training in the jungles of the Philippines and we arrived in Subic Bay to take them to Vietnam. There was time to go ashore, so I walked through the gates of the naval base into Philippine territory. While crossing over a small bridge, a toxic whiff of open sewers forced me to hold a handkerchief to my nose. I was now in Elongapo, a city which reminded me of Tijuana on the border of the U.S. and Mexico. Elongapo was evidently a place which prospered from the presence of large numbers of American servicemen. It had a reputation for lawlessness. A few days before our arrival, the mayor of Elongapo had been shot dead, as he walked on the street in broad daylight.

The crowded sidewalks were lined with bars, shops selling tacky curios, cheap shoes and highly-coloured shirts. Street vendors vied for space with touts offering tickets to sex shows. Taxi cabs and busses were painted in several colours and garishly decorated with gleaming brassware, and their proud drivers blew their horns continuously to attract attention. Thieves were active.

My attention was drawn to commotion among a group of American sailors who had come out of a bar. A gang of youths had staged a fight to divert attention and had skillfully slipped their fingers under the watch bands of some of the onlookers, and had made off with a few valuable timepieces. The angry sailors chased in vain as the kids disappeared into the crowd. When I returned aboard, the man at the gangway told me that one of our stewards had been enticed into a sleazy hotel, by a girl he met in a bar. He followed her into a squalid little room, and while he removed his clothes she disappeared behind a screen. Two men armed with knives appeared from behind the same screen and relieved him of his wallet and watch. So much for Elongapo. There was little to recommend it.

23

Losing it in South Korea

After we had been two months on the shuttle run I had a streak of bad luck. Jerry Boyd and I went ashore in Vung Tau. We sat in a crowded bar enjoying a cold beer, and I was careless enough to eat shell fish handed to me by an attentive girl, who picked these morsels of dubious quality out of the shells with a tooth pick. Whether this indiscretion was the cause of my illness I do not know. Jerry left to return aboard, while I walked along the dusty road to the outskirts of Vung Tau and wandered innocently into a village which I thought interesting. It was only later I learned that I had strayed into an area frequented by the Viet Cong. Unwanted visitors in this village often disappeared.

We were heading north in the Bashi Strait. I was on the 8 - midnight watch. We were due to arrive in Pusan the next day when I became ill. Doubled-up by excruciating stomach pains I was carried below to the ship's hospital, where the doctor told me that I had appendicitis. Dr. John Benn and I were friends. He had told me earlier about his trips to Canada, his plans to climb in the Rocky Mountains and his work ashore in Pusan, where he and his colleagues treated cases of hair lip and other easily corrected deformities. " I am not happy with the war in Vietnam and my involvement in it, but feel at least I can do something to help people in Korea who cannot get medical attention." Now I was his patient. He stuck an intravenous needle in my arm and said, " I thought of operating right away but will wait until we get to Pusan."

It was late afternoon before we docked. A stretcher party arrived to take me ashore accompanied by Dr. Benn. "Tony, there's a jeep waiting on the dock, the driver will take you to the 121st Evacuation hospital and I will remove your appendix tonight." The medics had a tough time lifting me up the steep ladder when I nearly slipped feet first out of the stretcher. On deck the heat was oppressive and although partly covered by a sheet I began to sweat. A large, cheering crowd had assembled to greet the returning soldiers. On reaching the dock I found myself being scrutinized by Koreans who must have wondered why I was the only person being removed by stretcher from the ship. As we made our way to the jeep a military band struck up a tune. "I bet you've never received a welcome like this." said the doctor in his humourous way. Sick as I felt I managed a laugh. "I am overwhelmed, never knew I was so popular. I hope they don't expect a speech, I 'm not dressed for the occasion. How far away is the hospital?" I asked, "I am dying of thirst." Dr. Benn adjusted the intravenous drip as I lay in the back of the jeep. " Its about ten miles out into the country. I will see you later. Have a good trip." A bottle of fluid hung on a steel pole beside me, and a tube led down to the needle in my arm.

*The 'General Gordon' in Pusan, waiting for troops
to embark.*

We drove off slowly through the throng until we passed out of the docks and into the streets of Pusan. I wondered when I would see the ship again. She was due to sail for Vietnam within 24 hours and there had been rumours of her returning to the States from there.

Before long we were out in the rich farmland which lay between Pusan and the mountains. It was a beautiful, warm twilight evening and farmers were still at work on their crops. Men guided their implements pulled by long- horned cows, while women, wearing coned shaped straw hats, worked with hoes. Children waved as we passed and I wished that I was sightseeing in different circumstances.

An armed guard stopped us at the entrance to the 121st Evacuation hospital, which looked more like a country club than a military establishment. A dozen or more small houses stood apart from the main building, each in its own plot of well-tended lawn and flower beds. Recollections of my stay there are hazy. I do remember coming to in the early hours of the next day and seeing Dr. Benn bending over me." Tony, how do you feel? There was nothing wrong with your appendix but I took it out anyway. I'm afraid that you will miss the ship. We sail today. You will have to stay here until they find out what's wrong with you."

The days that followed were hot and uncomfortable. I was alone, and except for the occasional visit from the nurse I saw no other patients. I was unable to hold down any food and constant vomiting was a source of embarrassment, but the Korean nurse was quite unperturbed. If not for her I would have been even more wretched. Her name was Ann Myo Cha. She was charming and kind. "My English and writing is No 10." She seemed to know what I needed and although I was too sick to eat, or sit up and read a book, at least I knew that someone cared about me. I had been forgotten, until the day I was told that I was to be sent back to the States. It now appeared that my job had come to an end; my spirits were very low.

24

A military hospital in Seoul

The flight to the States was to be via Seoul, the capital of South Korea. It turned out to be a very unusual trip. I was put on a stretcher and taken to a landing strip on the outskirts of Pusan; there were no planes or buildings in sight, merely a wind sock on a pole standing at the side of the runway. A few military vehicles stood nearby. My stretcher was taken from the ambulance and I was left on the grass under a blazing midday sun. I must have lain there in sweaty discomfort for the better part of an hour before hearing the buzz of an approaching plane. The twin-engined plane came to a stop and soon I was lifted aboard, through a door in the rear of the plane, where two smiling American nurses pushed me onto a shelf-like bunk against the side of the aircraft. The door was closed and soon the plane was bumping about over an uneven runway, before lifting up over the mountains surrounding Pusan. There was so little room in my bunk that I was unable to sit upright.

Up to then I was feeling sorry for myself but this ceased when I realized that the plane had just arrived from Vietnam and was full of war-wounded. There was a strong smell of antiseptic and the moans of wounded men. Feeling reluctant to make demands upon overworked nurses, I delayed asking for a means of passing water, but before we landed at Taegu to unload some of the wounded, my discomfort became urgent. I was given a receptacle for discharge, only to find to my chagrin, that it was impossible to use as I could not sit up. It was a great relief when we landed at Kimpo Airport, Seoul. It was dark by the time I arrived at the military hospital and was carried into a Nissen Hut full of wounded and sick American soldiers.

My stay in Pusan had been an ordeal, but the three weeks spent in the hospital in Seoul was made worse when I came under the care of a hardened male nurse called Hagen, who showed a streak of sadism in his ministrations. He must have hated his work because he certainly did not like his patients. He was a thick-set, bull-necked man in his mid-thirties, with short cropped bristly red hair and an aggressive manner. He was in charge of the ward during the night and it was in the early hours when I came to his attention. I was hot and uncomfortable, and because of the tube which had been stuck up my nose, I was having trouble breathing properly. In a frenzied attempt to get more air, I pulled the tube out. This was soon noticed by Hagen who began shouting as he came towards, me and with one hand pushed on my chest, and with the other grabbed the tube and pushed it roughly back up my nose. I put up some resistance to this sudden unseemly assault, and in the process the intravenous needle in my arm came out. This further enraged Hagen, he took hold of my arm in a vice-like grip, and grabbing the needle, he began prodding to find the vein. I yelled in protest, and just when things began to get out of hand the Korean nurse, who had just arrived on duty, came to my rescue. She bravely pushed Hagen aside and gently and skillfully inserted the needle back into my arm. With a few comforting words, none of which I understood, she made me feel that there was at least one Florence Nightingale left in the noble world of nursing.

The daylight hours were more bearable, thanks to the absence of the obnoxious Hagen, and I was beginning to settle down, until I looked in my bag of personal effects and discovered that my wallet was missing. Losing a few dollars was bad enough; more serious was the loss of my identity card.

In 1967 there were about 30,000 American troops defending the border between North and South Korea. The D.M.Z. Line was only 30 miles from Seoul, and soldiers were being killed and wounded in skirmishes between the opposing troops. In the bed next to mine was a badly wounded G.I. named Frank, who had just come round after an operation to repair the wound on his scalp, and although heavily bandaged and sedated, he was able to tell me what had happened.

He was in a work party and sitting next to the driver of the truck carrying a dozen soldiers to repair the fence, dividing the North and South. It was a dangerous operation and armed guards stood in the back of the truck with the other men. They were travelling in a convoy of trucks, and only a mile or two from base, when a North Korean soldier suddenly emerged from a ditch firing a recoilless rifle. The driver was killed instantly, Frank was hit in the head and two men in the back were badly wounded. Their truck landed on its side in the ditch and the survivors scrambled out. Frank didn't know what happened to their attacker. He woke up in here, in this hospital, and was now wondering whether he would be shipped back to the States.

The loss of my wallet had been reported to the military police and a security man came to interview me. I was in no fit state to answer probing questions as to my identity, and my interrogator seemed to get impatient when I tried to explain that I was a Canadian working aboard an American ship. He intended to contact the Canadian Consul to establish my identity but there was no such person in Seoul. The British Consul was asked to provide information however he was uncooperative, and just when I was about to be declared a displaced person the U.S. Navy in nearby Inchon came to my rescue. A friendly young lieutenant appeared at my bedside and vouched for my true identity.

Among the walking wounded was a lanky Texan called Wes. He hobbled on crutches between the beds and swore loudly when his progress was obstructed. I offered some words of encouragement expecting to receive an angry response, instead he seemed glad to receive attention and sat on the end of my bed. " I am counting the days until I get out of this godammed place. What's wrong with you, fella ?" he asked. I told him that I didn't know but was just as anxious to leave as he was. Wes lifted his right leg and I was shocked to see a heavily bandaged stump. "I lost my godammed foot, now I am waiting to go back to the States and be fitted with a new one. And sooner the better." "How did it happen? " I enquired, wondering whether it was insensitive to ask. But Wes seemed willing to talk about it," My outfit was clearing a village where the Viet-Cong had been holed up. We knew that the bastards had mined the area and we had to make a search. There was always a bunch of villagers watching us when we did this, we knew that they had been sheltering the Cong, and some of the guys were fidgety, had itchy fingers, and wanted to shoot them. As we swept the ground for mines we watched the kids who stood a safe distance away, because they knew where the mines were. They had seen them planted. So when a little girl suddenly covered her ears with her hands, we knew that we were near a mine and we usually found it. I was unlucky. I had had some close calls before and began to think I

107

would complete my time in Nam without getting hurt. I was sweeping around with a few other guys and when I put my right foot down I heard a click. For a fraction of a second I thought that if I held my foot down nothing would happen. I lost my foot but it could have been worse. The godammed war is over for me, now I can get the hell out of here."

The doctor on his daily rounds came to the conclusion that my inability to keep down food was caused by some obstruction and ordered X-rays to be taken. Swallowing a large glass of barium before each of these sessions took a long time and this irritated the nurse, who was in a hurry. After the third X-ray the doctor had a frown on his face. " It doesn't look good." he said " You have a blockage in the stomach, it may be malignant, but we will take another X-ray to make sure." This news was unsettling to say the least. After the X-ray the doctor approached my bed smiling, "Good news." he said. "Whatever it was, it has disappeared. We are sending you back to your ship." I felt like a man reprieved from a death sentence. As luck would have it the *General Gordon* was due back in Pusan in two days. Only one problem remained. As my wallet had been stolen, I had no money to pay for the air fare. Navy Lieutenant John Fehn came to see me again. He must have known I needed help, and being a generous fellow he lent me $100 out of his own pocket. My return flight to Pusan was more comfortable than the previous one to Seoul.

25

Returning home

I was delighted to return aboard the ship and celebrated my recovery by going ashore with David Johnstone, who insisted on paying for the drinks. News came that we were returning to the States. The authorities had decided that it was more practical to bring the troops home by air, and we sailed with only a handful of military personnel aboard. Among them was a helicopter pilot who had refused to return home by plane. His nerves had been shattered after two horrifying crashes, when he was carrying troops, and his craft had been brought down by enemy fire. After the second crash the crew scrambled out of the wreckage and were mown down by withering fire. He was the only survivor and vowed that he would never fly again.

On the stern, a large pen had been built to house two monitor lizards bound for a zoo in the States. These lizards, 12 feet long, had ferocious jaws and a fearsome reputation. We were warned not to fraternize with them, as they were carnivorous and one could lose a finger or two offering tidbits through the wire mesh.

On reaching Oakland I learned that my job had come to an end. The officer who had delivered the letter said that the M.S.T.S. needed mates on their cargo ships and they would gladly have sent me to one, but the Coast Guard regulations would not allow non- residents to be in charge on the bridge of an American ship.

I was looking forward to going home with a wad of greenbacks in my pocket and heard of a way to travel back to Canada without spending money on a plane ticket. An agency in San Francisco needed drivers to deliver cars around the country. All I had to do was show a valid drivers license, make a deposit of $200 and enjoy a holiday on the road. Fortunately a car had to be delivered to Bellingham, Washington, which is within a few miles of the Canadian border. I had hoped it would be a small economy car but I was given the keys to a monstrous black Lincoln Continental. Feeling like a mafia boss I sank into the well upholstered seat of this oversized machine and gingerly manoeuvred it out onto the busy streets. After making several wrong turns I finally found the Golden Gate Bridge and headed north in splendid luxury. All went well until I reached the coastal town of Crescent Beach, where I was stopped by the Highway Patrol who were inspecting vehicles for possible defects. To my surprise the black juggernaut did not achieve a clean sheet. According to the gruff patrolman, the Lincoln tended to move forward when in neutral but I was allowed to drive away, after signing the card and promising to fix the defect within a month. On delivering the car to a dealer in Bellingham, I boarded a bus for Canada, and home.

It was March 20th 1968. I had been away for thirteen months. A month later I received a letter from Jerry Boyd, the 2nd mate of the *General Gordon*. He had been transferred to the troopship *General Geiger*. At first he was quite content as she seemed to be a happy ship, but at mid Pacific, soon after Christmas, a tragedy cast a cloud of gloom over the ship. The chief mate, who was highly regarded by everyone, jumped overboard. He left a note which said that he had "reached the end of the line."

After a decent spell at home I found a job in Vancouver as 2nd mate on a rail boxcar carrier. She was really a self-propelled barge and an uglier vessel would be hard to find. I found it difficult to adjust to life aboard and had no intention of staying. This job would do until I could find something more to my liking. The *Doris Yorke* was a vessel of about 1000 tons driven by two noisy Caterpillar diesels and capable of 11 knots. She was fairly new and something of a novelty on the coast because she had an upper deck on which cars could be loaded by means of an elevator.

I was prejudiced against the ship from the very beginning because I hated the 6 hours on, 6 hours off system, and this dislike was reinforced when I encountered some hostility among the crew. My first night aboard was enough to tempt me to walk ashore. I had been on watch from 1800 to midnight, during which I tried to master the system of loading and had unwittingly held up the operation by my ignorance of the way things were supposed to work. This angered the master who began to shout at me and he seemed perilously close to having a heart attack.

When I finally reached my cabin after being relieved by the mate, I was near exhaustion and collapsed on my bunk hoping to find relief in slumber. It was not to be. Loading continued and the screech of box car wheels, the rumble of the lifting machinery and the lurch of the *Doris Yorke* from one side to the other made rest impossible. I had nostalgic thoughts of the *General Gordon* and the life I had just left, and cursed the turn of events which had landed me on this rotten ship.

Before the month was over I packed my bags, left the ship and went home. My habit of going from job to job seems to have caused some disquiet among my older children, who had remarked that, " Dad never stays in one job for very long." They wondered why the fathers of their friends had good jobs and were always at home. They had good reason to criticize me; I had lost count of the jobs I had had since coming to Canada. But feelings of guilt were offset by the knowledge that, despite my erratic record, I had never failed to " put the bacon on the table." Nevertheless I was stung by the truth of what they said and attempted to explain to them my belief that there was no point in staying in a job if one didn't like it. I got the impression that they found that argument unconvincing. I was now forty-eight years old, an age when most men had settled down in a steady job and a comfortable life at home. Surely I could do the same. But it was to be a few more years before I found that sort of job.

26

The *Northland Prince*

After a few days leave I found a job with the Northland Navigation Company which owned half a dozen coastal ships. My first job was 3rd mate of the *Northern Prince*, a coaster of about 700 tons which had been under the Norwegian flag. After a trip to the Queen Charlotte Islands, during which I readjusted to coastal seafaring, I was promoted to 2nd mate of the company flagship, the *Northland Prince*. When times were good the company had built this cargo ship of 3000 tons. She was a handsome, single screw ship, 329 feet long, powered by a Stork diesel, capable of 15 knots and with accommodation for 100 passengers. She was designed for the coastal trade from Vancouver to ports on the coast, and her terminal port was the mining town of Stewart, some 100 miles north of Prince Rupert.

I hadn't been aboard long before I realized that I was back in the sort of shipboard existence I had endured earlier in coastal ships. A high pressure sort of seafaring that existed in the Union Company and White Pass ships. Although the Northland Navigation was partly subsidised by the government, competition with other companies was fierce and the company had to make money or go out of business. Therefore there was a great haste to load the ship in Vancouver and have her back on her way north. This urgency produced a certain tension aboard, particularly in port when the deck crew worked feverishly to load and unload the ship as quickly as possible.

The wages were good, and the accommodation and food excellent, but this was not enough to make a happy ship. From past experience I found that it never was and, as always, the human element was lacking. Aboard the *Northland Prince* there was constant bickering between the captain and the deck officers, and a state of war between them and the seamen and their union. This lack of harmony aboard made life miserable and it was a great relief when, after three weeks, it was time to go home on a weeks leave.

'The Northland Prince' entering Vancouver harbour.

The master was a square jawed, thick set, red haired man in his mid-forties who seemed to be in a perpetual state of bad temper. As a junior mate I didn't expect the master to be friendly, he was there to run a ship, and friendship with the officers wasn't a requirement for his job. But respect was lacking for a man who treated his officers badly. No matter how hard we tried it was never enough to please him. Whenever his face turned red it was the signal that he was about to have an apoplectic fit and explode with fury. It was unfortunate that at such times he suffered from a slight speech impediment, and while his lips moved nothing intelligible moved passed them for a few seconds, then the gears of speech connected and out came a torrent of invective and abuse. His temper was at a peak in port. While working to load or discharge the cargo on the main deck, we mates could see him pacing up and down on the bridge working himself up into a frenzy of impatience. Sometimes he would give a blast on the ship's horn to

113

register his anger, and I knew that once we sailed I would have to go to the bridge and offer some explanation for any perceived delay. However reasonable, it was never good enough to satisfy him.

The seamen were divided into two camps. There were those who seemed intent on causing trouble. These were men who carried the union rule book in their pockets and would call a stoppage of work on the slightest pretext, real or imagined. There were others who just wanted to get the job done, particularly if we were working in wretched conditions, such as ice on the dock in a blizzard. And there was a question of unsafe working practices. We had done this sort of job many times before and unpleasant as it was, any delay only prolonged the agony.

Common sense should have prevailed but all too often it didn't, and conflict and confrontation became the accepted way of doing things except when the 1st mate was on deck. Bud Cole was a tough man and the malcontents didn't mess with him. His job at sea was secondary to his real interest ashore, which was running a chicken farm in the Fraser Valley. He didn't need to go to sea, it was merely a profitable diversion. He was an easy going, pleasant man and a very efficient mate. Of medium height and broad shouldered, he was the strongest man on the ship. Nobody argued with him, not even the old man. He knew his job better than most men and when he was on deck the work progressed without a hitch.

Bud Cole was always able to find a solution to a problem. He reminded me of Borge Bentzen, the mate of the Waikawa with whom I had sailed in 1950; a human dynamo who riled the crew because he worked harder than anyone. Unlike some cargo ships, where the officers were not expected to perform any physical labour, the mates aboard the Northland Navigation ships worked alongside the crew. They were expected to wear their uniforms when on the bridge and in the ship's saloon, but if a mate on joining the ship thought that he would never get his hands dirty, he was wrong. Bud Cole was not the sort of man who was content to stand by and watch, he worked alongside the men, and, being anxious to pull my weight, I did the same. I found that there was always something to learn by watching him.

One day we were unloading trucks from No.2 hold onto the dock in Stewart, a port on the Canadian Alaskan border. The tide was at its lowest and there was not enough drift on the wire runner to lift one truck over the bull rail and on to the dock. It seemed to me that we would have to wait for the rising tide, but the mate was a man with a lot of cargo handling experience. He ordered the seaman to put wire slings under a heavy load of chain lying on deck at No 3 hatch. The chain was lifted and swung over the side of the ship opposite to the dock; this listed the ship sufficiently to bring the truck clear of the bull rail. It was landed without delay.

27

Into the 'drink' again

Not all of the men were discontented. Ray Price was the best seaman on deck. He had sailed deep sea on Canadian Park ships and was the sort of man who could tackle any job. I was always glad to have him on my watch. Ray was tough and the malcontents didn't bother him. He had the sense to know that the job was a well paid one. Why kill the goose that laid the golden egg? It was by no means certain that the government subsidy would last much longer, and if it was withdrawn we would all be out of a job. Ray had a close call one trip when we were steaming up the Douglas Channel bound for Kitimat.

Lifeboat drill aboard the 'Northland Prince'. I am wondering if someone put in the plug.

The *old man* ordered a lifeboat drill and Ray was one of the seamen in my boat crew. The intention was to swing the boat out but not to lower it into the water, as the ship was steaming at full speed. Ray got into the boat and I ordered it to be lifted off the chocks and swung out. The boats were lifted on hooks at the bow and stern by chain links which hung from the davit. I had failed to notice that the link at the bow was precariously balanced on the tip of the hook. The slightest jar was enough to dislodge it; the bow dropped, and Ray was thrown into the icy water.

A life ring was thrown over, the *old man* on the bridge gave the order to swing our stern away from the man overboard. The ship was stopped, another boat was lowered and Ray was picked up within 10 minutes of going overboard. He was put into a hot shower and being tough, was none the worse for his unexpected immersion. He had good reason to complain about my failure to see the wayward hook, but he never said a word.

28

A discontented captain and crew

Another seaman, Pancho Gonzalez, was a happy fellow who never complained. He seemed to enjoy his job, especially when driving a forklift on the dock. He was always in a hurry, thus earning the nickname "Speedy Gonzalez." He remained silent whenever a dispute erupted, not wishing to offend anyone. He had left Mexico for a better life in Canada, and with a family to support he was content to have a job and couldn't understand why some men didn't feel as he did.

And there was Mickey Jenny. A good seaman. He lived in a make believe world of fantasy; a double life. Aboard, he was Mickey the seaman, ashore he was Mickey the millionaire. Some of the men made fun of him when he droned on about it. They had heard it all dozens of times. His stories didn't bore me when he was at the wheel during my watch, and we were running in open waters. There was time to chat. Occasionally I would put in a word, but Mickey wasn't listening. He spoke about his private plane which whisked him off to exotic lands of yachts and mansions in Europe. How he managed to travel so far and wide in the space of a week's leave no one knew. He spoke of his daughters, who he referred to as 'the twins'. The sad truth was that as far as anyone knew, Mickey had no children, no great wealth, and lived by himself in rooming house in the run down East End of Vancouver. He had a postal number as an address. It was only later that I realized that he had a split personality. I liked him because he did his job and never complained.

I was as anxious as the other mates to get the job done as quickly as possible but in doing so, I unwittingly fell victim to the intrigues of some of the men. We were homeward bound and in Bella Bella which was the last port of call before Vancouver. It was during the midnight to four watch. The mate had told me earlier that there was no need to call out any seamen who were off watch and asleep. Our watch could handle the cargo as only one hatch would be opened. As always, the master was in a temper and as I left the bridge to go on deck he told me that he would not tolerate any delays. It was always the same, as if he expected me to loiter.

When the last load was about to be landed on deck, the winchman allowed it to swing. The two seaman with me were having trouble steadying it. I placed my hand on the load in an innocent effort to assist and thought nothing more about it.

We reached Vancouver next day and I was summoned to the office to be confronted by an irate marine superintendent. He demanded to know why all the seamen had put in for an hours overtime during our stop at Bella Bella. "Why did you need all the seaman on deck when only one hatch was working?" he said, waving a piece of paper in my face. "Every godammed man is on this overtime sheet."

For a moment I wondered what he was talking about. "I didn't call any men who were off watch" I spluttered defensively. But someone had conspired against me. My action in steadying the load was not seen as being helpful, but a deliberate attempt to avoid overtime. Because of this, men who were asleep in their bunks were entitled to overtime, and the company had to pay it. I thought it a contemptible action which almost cost me my job. The tensions of the job were beginning to tell. I wondered how much longer I could stick it out.

29

Grievous bodily harm

Working cargo had its hazards. In our haste to finish the job we often took chances at some cost to our safety. On one occasion, when the ship was in Stewart, I was standing in the tween deck as the car cage was being lowered into the hold. It held a three ton Cadillac. As I was steadying it to clear the side of the hatch coaming, the winchman let some slack on the wire runner and one of my fingers was broken when caught between the cage and the coaming. A taxi took me to the only doctor in town who made temporary repairs. On another occasion I was working in the lower hold, when the wheel of a towmotor went over my foot. Fortunately no bones were broken. More damage to my person was to occur later.

When the decks were covered in ice and the hatches were open, conditions became difficult. One bitterly cold day we were unloading cargo at the dock in Vancouver, I was in the tween decks of No 2 hold and in a hurry as usual. A canvas chute hung over the hatch and led down into the lower hold to extract the fumes made by the towmotor working there. Holding a cargo manifest in one hand I moved quickly along the deck and slipped on a patch of ice. Thinking that the chute was a solid steel stanchion, I clutched it in an effort to stop falling and plummeted 17 feet into the lower hold.

With blood oozing out of my mouth and nose I lay motionless, until the somewhat surprised longshoremen gathered me up and laid me on a pallet board for immediate discharge. The longshoremen must have wondered why I hadn't bothered to use the ladder! I came to in an ambulance on the way to St Paul's hospital. I had broken my heel bone, left wrist bone, cheek bone and two ribs. I was laid-up for seven weeks of enforced idleness and when I did return to work it was with the resolution to go about my duties with more care.

30

The price of loyalty

During the summer months the regular seamen took their annual leave. Sometimes they were replaced by misfits. At the beginning of one trip, I had the misfortune to have one on my watch. As usual we sailed shortly before midnight and after we had cleared the Lion's Gate bridge, the Master handed the watch over to me and went below. I was now alone with a relief seamen at the wheel; his name was Hogan. The stand-by seaman, a regular member of the crew, was on deck helping the other men tighten the lashings on our deck cargo. I thought I got a whiff of liquor in the vicinity of Hogan, but it wasn't until I glanced at the compass that I knew that something was amiss. He was 15 degrees off course.

Thinking that perhaps he had been given the wrong course I gave him the correct one, then turned to look at the chart. A minute later I turned around to see the ship turning rapidly towards the land. I pushed Hogan aside and grabbed the wheel, corrected the swing and put the ship back on course. I didn't have to ask him what was wrong, for as soon as he opened his mouth I knew he was drunk. A short blast on the whistle brought the stand-by seaman to the bridge (not in the Rules of the Road, but sometimes used to summon a seaman) and I told Hogan to take the wheel, "You are fired," I said "Go below. You are no use up here." He shouted and swore in protest saying that he knew his job and who was I to tell him otherwise. With some persuasion he left the bridge muttering threats about revenge.

We had only left Vancouver an hour earlier, and it might have been better to have returned to the dock, put the him ashore and call for another seaman. But where would we have got a replacement in the middle of the night? We would have lost six or more hours and neither the master or the company would have tolerated that. We now had the problem of carrying a useless seaman for the trip. He was to cause trouble later during the trip but fortunately not on my watch.

Everyone was pleased to see the back of him when we returned to Vancouver.

A week later we were back in Vancouver and still discharging cargo in the early hours of the morning. I was on watch and looking forward to going home that day for a week's leave. The window in my room overlooked the foredeck and I had gone there to do some paperwork. My attention was suddenly focused on a figure coming up the gangway. It was Hogan, the man who had been fired two weeks earlier. I sensed trouble and hurried down on deck and into the crew's messroom to find Hogan with a cup in hand. He was talking to three seamen.

"What are you doing aboard?" I asked. He put his cup down and eyed me ominously. "Just having a coffee and a chat with the boys. There's no problem, mate." Hogan was a big fellow with an ugly expression. It seemed to me that he wasn't on friendly terms with any of the crew, and therefore had no reason to be aboard. " I want you off the ship in five minutes. Finish your coffee and go." I said, trying to conceal feelings of apprehension.

I returned to my room wondering whether I had been wise in allowing him to stay that long. I became engrossed with the job on hand then realized that I must make sure that Hogan had gone ashore. I returned to the messroom to find Hogan now sitting down to a meal. "I thought I told you leave. Get to hell off this ship." I had hardly got the words out when Hogan stood up, sprang forward and hit me in the face. I fell backwards over a bench and landed on the deck.

This was not the first time I had come under fire in the course of doing my duty. I had been hit on the nose two trips earlier by a seaman who I had found asleep on duty, and he took exception to my disturbing his rest. I pondered the fact that over the past twenty years I had been attacked three times, (once in a lifeboat in Auckland Harbour). I wasn't a particularly pugnacious person, what was it about me that aroused such passions? Perhaps I possessed the sort of face that men liked to thump. It was a disquieting thought; a face that, in the past, had provoked men to hit me. Perhaps being of short stature was a disadvantage.

One of the seamen, Andy Thomas, a native Indian with whom I got along well, rushed to my aid and began grappling with Hogan, who managed to free himself and run out of the messroom. Holding a handkerchief to my bloodied face I staggered out on deck after him, to be met by the cargo foreman who had come to find out what all the commotion was about. "Call the Police" I shouted, trying to regain some composure as I pushed past curious longshoremen.

Two men of the Vancouver Harbour Patrol were soon on the scene. "Get into the car." said the sergeant. "Who attacked you?" While I sat in the back giving details of the event, the constable driving the car picked up the phone and began relaying information to the police head quarters. As we drove along the road past La Pointe Pier, the sergeant directed a searchlight among the railroad wagons and along the dark alleys between grain elevators. The radio crackled and information came back from police headquarters. Terry Hogan was an alias, his real name was Jack Chapman. He was well known to police and wanted for assault, trespassing, possession of stolen goods and resisting arrest.

Suddenly the beam of light caught a figure running between boxcars. "There he is." said the sergeant picking up the phone to speak to a second police car which had joined the chase. Within minutes Chapman was in handcuffs and being bundled into the other car. "He denies all knowledge of the charge," said the policeman walking up from the car behind us. "He says that he has never heard of you."

A few minutes later the constable returned. "It's a different story now. He admits striking you and wants to apologize. Mr. Winstanley do you wish to press charges?" Still smarting from the assault I replied" Yes, I do. I am sick of being punched up while doing my job."

"Don't blame you," said the constable scribbling on his notebook, "You are right. We get tired of complainants who are beaten up and then decide to drop charges." He picked up the phone and relayed the information to headquarters. " You will have to go to court in the morning."

"But I am going on leave tomorrow." I protested, "I need a rest." It was now 3 a.m., I had been away from the ship for over an hour and wondered what was going on aboard without an officer on deck.

It is quite remarkable how the law can sometimes bend the rules to fit the need. A Justice of the Peace was roused from his bed and he appeared bleary eyed but uncomplaining at the Police Headquarters. I signed the necessary document charging Chapman with assault.

By the time I returned to the ship it was dawn and the Port of Vancouver was preparing for another busy day. After filling in the logbook and reporting the nights events to the officer who relieved me, I went home to Victoria. As for Hogan alias Chapman he was sentenced to three months, or a $500 fine, and since he had no money or friends to pay it, he spent time in the pokey for the dubious pleasure of bashing me in the face.

As the weeks dragged on I became more disenchanted with my job. The only time when life aboard the *Northland Prince* became tolerable, was when the master went on leave and his place was taken by Captain Emile Villeneuve. Captain Villeneuve was a quiet, unflappable man who left the mates alone to get on with the job. When the regular master returned, the abuse and fault finding continued. I knew that sooner or later there would be a confrontation between us. I had to be sure that I was in the right when this happened. An opportunity came sooner than expected.

Aboard ship the unwritten law dictates that when a master has cause to reprimand an officer, he does so in private and not in front of the crew. We were working cargo in Prince Rupert; I had gone to the bridge for some reason, only to be waylaid by the master, who began a tirade about something on deck which was not to his liking. Two seamen happened to be standing nearby. The master, his arms akimbo and with a defiant expression on his face, was half way through his diatribe when I took the bull by the horns. Stepping forward I shouted "Captain, I've had enough of your constant criticism. If you have something to say to me it must be in the privacy of your room."

Shaking with anger and apprehension I wondered whether I was about to be hit, fired or both. Strangely, the master's expression changed. For once, his face didn't go red. He was taken aback and with an altered tone of voice, said " I will see you in my room at the end of your watch."

Feeling some satisfaction that at last I had forced him to back down, I decided to keep him waiting for a few minutes. As I entered his room, I wondered what sort of reception I would receive. The transformation was remarkable. He spoke softly and began by telling me that he wouldn't tolerate insubordination from officers, but in the same breath added that everyone was under strain and all he wanted was to run a good ship with a happy crew. From that day on he never bothered me again. He made an almost complete turn-about; he was polite and at times even humorous.

My days aboard the *Northland Prince* were now numbered. Labour strife escalated, and soon after our arrival in Vancouver the unhappy crew went on strike, in sympathy with the equally discontented longshoremen. "The company are a greedy bunch of bastards." announced seaman, sea lawyer Gerry Holt. He sat in the messroom, dressed in his shore going gear, gulping down his third cup of coffee and patting his ample belly. "The company pockets all the profits and all we get are the droppings."

The crew walked ashore. I wondered what to do as I was now off pay. It was time to look for another job. Don Robson, the 3rd mate, was optimistic. "I'm not worried." he said." I will go back to the towboats, I've had enough of cargo ships. Tony, you should try the ferries, they say it's a good outfit to work for and you will get home every night." Any thoughts I had of going to work in ferries was anathema. I remembered the dark days in the mid- fifties when I worked in ships owned by the C.P.R. I had formed a prejudice against ferries of any kind. However, a pleasant surprise awaited me.

31

Discovering British Columbia Ferries

I boarded the bus for the B.C. Ferries Terminal at Horseshoe Bay, a picturesque spot on Howe Sound about 20 miles from Vancouver. It proved to be a good decision. The personnel manager offered me a cup of coffee saying, " Yes, there is a 2nd officers job available in one of our major vessels. Are you available to start work tomorrow?"

Any pessimism I felt before joining the ferries was swept away. " Yes, of course." I replied, hardly believing this fortuitous turn of events. "You will only be a temporary employee," said the manager glancing at my discharge book. "But you can count on work until the end of the summer season. After that some of our fleet will be laid-up for the winter. You will get over two months work." The terms of employment made me wonder why I hadn't applied earlier. They were good wages, ten days work and then five days off; almost too good to be true. Where else could a man go to sea during the day, yet be home every night? It was ideal, especially as my daughter and her husband lived a few miles from the terminal and they were generous enough to offer me a room in their home.

How wonderful it was to find myself aboard a ship with friendly officers and crew, doing a job free of tension and in so doing, the mates never got their hands dirty. My first ship was the *Queen of New Westminster*, 6000 gross tons, twin screw, speed 18 knots. She carried about 200 cars and trucks and 1000 passengers. She ran between the mainland and Nanaimo on Vancouver Island.

At first it wasn't all smooth sailing, as one incident illustrates. This occasion upset the tranquility of a summer's evening crossing of the Gulf of Georgia. It was my first day aboard and I was on watch when we cleared Entrance Island bound for Horseshoe Bay. I gave the quartermaster the course which would take us across the Gulf of Georgia. A few minutes later, noticing that he had strayed off track I asked him what course he was steering?

He answered, " I am steering on the ski lift" (a line of lights clearly visible on Hollyburn Mountain above West Vancouver). Flabbergasted I said, "You are doing what?" He repeated himself in a truculent manner, which I took as his rebuke to a new mate who didn't know the local customs. "I'm steering the usual course, on the ski lift, it's easy to see."

It was necessary to remind him that I had given him a compass course and he must steer it but he was not easily convinced. He had done nothing wrong; he had spent four years in the ferries and knew what was best. New mates should be grateful for the knowledge he had to offer. After listening to this enlightening speech, I told him that unless he did as he was told, I would take it as a refusal to obey an order and the master would be informed. That was the end of the matter.

A few days later I found myself in trouble. Having been in ships where room and board was part of the job, I was not accustomed to having to pay for snacks and was most surprised when the captain waylaid me as I left the dining room. "Mr. Winstanley, It has come to my notice that you are taking doughnuts from the cafeteria and not paying for them." Thinking that perhaps I might wiggle out of this predicament by ridiculing his accusation, I said, " Yes Captain but I was only testing one to see whether it came up to company standards." This feeble attempt to blunt his charge did not move him." This practice has to stop or I shall take action." Feeling suitably deflated I retired to safer ground and from that time on, no doughnuts were unpaid for, and I soon settled down to enjoy a job which progressed with a minimum of fuss or stress.

At the end of the summer season my job came to an end. I was not unduly worried as I it appeared likely that I could return to the ferries in the spring. Now I had to find employment for the winter. After a spell at home I found a job which would take me into warmer climes.

32

West Indian Interlude

In mid-November I flew south to Mobile, Alabama to join a 47,000 deadweight tons, bulk carrier owned by the Reynolds Aluminum Co. of Richmond, Virginia. It was after mid-night when I got out of the taxi and looked up at the massive black hull, which the taxi driver insisted was the ship I was looking for. There was no sign of life aboard; she was in total darkness. A wooden ladder hung over her side and I wondered how I would get my baggage aboard. Thinking that perhaps I had come to the wrong ship I walked along the dock to read the name on the stern; she was the J. *Louis* of Monrovia (A Liberian registered ship), and I was her new 3rd mate.

Leaving my baggage on the dock I climbed aboard and walked aft where a dim light shone from a port-hole. After tripping over almost invisible ropes and wires strewn across the deck, I found the door to the accommodation and walked into the crews messroom. A West Indian seaman was stretched out asleep on a settee, he opened his eyes, disturbed by my entry. " I am the new 3rd mate" I said, by way of introduction. He sat up and said,. "Nobody tell me to expect a new mate. My name is Eric. I have worked all day man." "Well Eric, that maybe so, but I need your help now to bring my bags aboard."

I looked at the heap of dirty dishes lying on the table and it brought to mind conditions I had seen aboard many deep- sea ships. Eric rose slowly to his feet," Well man, I have a heaving line here for the very purpose of bringing your gear aboard." He shuffled out on deck carrying a lamp and I followed him. Then we proceeded to follow a process I hadn't seen since pre-war days aboard the old *Mandalay*; I went down on to the dock, Eric threw a heaving line over the side and securing the end to my heavy bag, heaved it aboard. He then led me along the dim and dingy alleyway, past cabins from which there came the sounds of men asleep, or half awake. We ascended a ladder to the officer's accommodation; it was austere and cheerless.

I hadn't expected luxury or a welcome of any kind but was annoyed to find my room in disarray, as if the previous occupant had left in a hurry. A heap of books, papers, and magazines covered the desk. Clothing was scattered across the deck, the bunk was unmade and bed linen lay in a rumpled heap. I was too tired to rouse the steward and demand clean linen so, throwing the bedding aside, I found a blanket, climbed onto the bunk and within seconds was asleep.

I was roused early next day by the steward who told me that officials from the City of Mobile Health Department were aboard, the crew had mustered in the officers' messroom and my presence was required. I joined a line of men and asked one of them the reason for the muster. "They are blaming us West Indian boys for an outbreak of V.D. in town." he said irritably. " They are looking in the wrong place. It's not us who is to blame, they just pickin on us man. And me a married man."

Two officials sat at the table marking the crew list. Nearby a doctor was jabbing a needle into the buttock of a cook who evidently objected to this affront to his dignity. " Why do you do this to me? I don't even go ashore in Mobile. Hell man, I don't even like your town or your women." The doctor's face wore an impassive expression and he merely waved him away. Then it was my turn. "What's your name?" said the official gruffly. "I am the new 3rd mate. I have just arrived from Canada." I replied jauntily, confident of my immunity to all foreign diseases. " Makes no difference mate, our orders are to treat everybody, and that's the whole crew." he said, with the tone of authority which brooks no argument. " But this is ridiculous, I have just come aboard." I raised my voice in despair, fearing that any objection was futile. " Drop your pants." ordered the man in white, " I don't have all day to waste." Aware that any further delay might jeopardize my job I complied. A sharp jab with a long needle didn't improve my temper; it was a rude introduction to a ship. The optimism I felt on arrival had sagged a bit.

The potency of the anti-biotic must have been sufficient to fell a horse, for next morning a part of me was paralysed and I had difficulty walking. The master, being a sympathetic man, ordered a taxi to take me to the company doctor. Dr. Hernandez was indignant. " Its typical of those fellas in the Port Health, you should write a letter of complaint. Here take these pills, they will fix you up." I did as he suggested and wrote a letter of protest. I received no reply.

I soon recovered the use of my legs and went about my duties. We sailed that evening and I felt relieved when the lights of Mobile disappeared astern. I had been away from deep sea ships for over ten years and it was necessary to remember the required procedures when leaving port. Fortunately my memory hadn't deserted me, nothing went amiss and soon we were out into the Gulf of Mexico bound for Ocho Rios, Jamaica.

With 10,000 tons of water ballast the ship made 17 knots, and the following day the Cayman Islands were sighted fine on the starboard bow. Captain Ebanks came on the bridge as I was plotting our position on the chart. " There's my home." he said, pointing to Little Cayman four miles on our starboard beam. He was a friendly man; we had met earlier in his room, where he had inspected my discharge book and seemed satisfied that I had plenty of watchkeeping experience. " We are a seafaring people. Most of the seamen from the Islands work aboard bulkers owned by Ludwig (National Bulk Carriers), or the Reynolds Company. But it won't be long before our jobs go to seamen from Asia, as they will work for half the wages."

Captain Ebanks told me about the attack on the J. Louis a year ago when she was off the coast of Cuba. " We were in International waters and over 40 miles off the coast, when a lone jet fighter, of the Cuban Air Force, flew low and gave us a burst of machine gun fire. One of the shells tore through the port lifeboat davit, you can see the hole from here. I guess he mistook our Liberian flag for the Stars and Stripes. We sent out a report and soon afterwards three U.S Air force planes appeared, but by then there was no sign of the Cuban plane. This is an American owned ship but we do not expect the same protection as we would get under the American flag."

It was hot and muggy in Ocho Rios, Jamaica. We began to load bauxite that was mined some 20 miles inland and carried on, what was reputed to be, the longest conveyor belt in the world. It ran over mountains and through forest to the loading dock. The J. Louis was a self-loading/discharging ship. The bauxite was fed into a shuttle at the ship's stern, where it dropped onto the ship's own conveyor belts which ran forward to the cavernous holds. These belts were 4 feet in width, and the system was capable of handling 2000 tons of bauxite an hour.

The loading was controlled by an operator sitting in a tower near the shuttle, and it was his job to ensure that the bauxite was evenly distributed throughout the ship. The loading dock was situated across the bay from the town and when loading was in progress and the wind blew from the west, a cloud of rust coloured bauxite dust reached the luxury hotels built for the burgeoning tourist trade. There were angry protests from tourists, as they lay beside the swimming pools basking in the sun and wondering why they were getting a tan so quickly.

To escape the noise and dust of loading I went ashore in Ocho Rios, walking past the hotels and into the busy, run-down part of the town. Along the main road were ramshackle shops with tin roofing and plaster walls covered in graffiti. Over the entrance to a red bricked hall a sign read, " Rude boys and bad men keep out. Law and order must prevail at all times. God save the Queen."

I met two of our engineers. They were haggling over the price of wood carvings of people and animals. I was about to buy one but Arnold Wegger, the German 3rd engineer said, "Wait until you go to Haiti. The carvings are better there."

I had, begun to settle aboard the J. Louis when to my surprise I was told to pack my bags. A message from the office had instructed me to proceed to Corpus Christi and join the Richard which was in need of a 3rd mate. The company car had arrived on the dock in Ocho Rios to take me to the airport at Montego Bay, some thirty miles away. "My name is Thomas." said the chauffeur smiling. He wore a straw hat and T shirt with a map of Jamaica printed on it." I take you to Montego by the scenic route man. You are lucky, I am the best driver in Jamaica."

With this assurance I settled into the back seat, sweat pouring down my face after the exertion of lugging my bags off the ship. The trip proved to be a wild one. We set off at high speed in a cloud of dust, scattering pedestrians, dogs and fowl in our wake. Then began the game of chicken which was a popular sport among drivers on the island. When another car appeared ahead, Thomas, instead of keeping to the left hand side of the road, deliberately steered directly at the oncoming car. When collision seemed imminent he would fling the car to the left, seconds before the other car hurtled past us. " Right on, you are chicken man." shouted Thomas triumphantly as if he was playing cricket and had hit a six over the pavilion. I sat transfixed by this madness, then recovering from shock and a tendency to evacuate I shouted," You can stop the car now, I will get out, find another taxi and report you to the office." Thomas was contrite and slowing down said, " O.K. man relax, I just having fun." I was beginning to understand the islander's carefree attitude to life; Jamaica has the sort of climate which induces a laid -back society. We drove at a more leisurely pace along the coast and I began to enjoy the passing scene of fine beaches, swaying coconut palms and sleepy villages.

33

The *Richard*

I boarded a Jamaica Air plane at Montego Bay and three hours later I emerged from the airport at Corpus Christi. I was met by a company minion, detailed to make sure I went straight to the ship at the Reynolds Aluminium dock about 10 miles south of the city.

The 'Richard'. An ugly but efficient ship

The *Richard* was a bulk carrier of 45,000 tons deadweight, 765 foot long, with a single screw powered by a steam turbine. She was built in the mid-sixties in Kure, Japan. She was an ugly brute of a ship, utilitarian built, with a stumpy funnel on the stern, and the bridge amidships tacked on by the builders almost as an afterthought. Still as a mover of cargo she was very efficient. The master's accommodation was below the bridge and next to the officer's dining saloon. He lived in splendid isolation amidships while the rest of us lived in the stern.

However he did share the dining-room with the chief engineer who walked forward for his meals.

Captain McCoy, a tall, bushy haired man in khaki uniform, was a Cayman Islander. The mate was a Yugoslav named Zeljko Ivacic, in his mid-thirties, a university graduate who spoke fractured English. I liked Zeljko; he was a hard working man, an excellent seaman, but he had a disconcerting way of addressing me. He was apt to say, "My dear Anton, I have a job for you. I like you to write letter to head office for me." I was happy to oblige but had to explain to him that it was not customary to address fellow officers as "My dear," the crew might not understand it. I was sure the Marine Superintendent in Corpus Christi would not appreciate reading a letter which began, " My dear Captain."

Lloyd Henry, the 2nd mate, was from Jamaica. There was another 3rd mate beside myself, Petar Stjopic, a 22 year old Yugoslav who stood the 8 to 12 watch. I was put on the middle watch (12 to 4). The engineers were from Spain, Germany and Barbados. The two engineers from Spain were Basques; hard faced men who at meal times sat together, but never uttered a word to each other or anyone else. The chief steward was Japanese and the radio officer was English. Our crew was a veritable league of nations, and remarkable as it may seem I got along well with everyone, with the exception of the radioman. He bore out the truth of G. B. Shaw's remark that, "It is impossible for an Englishman to open his mouth without making some other Englishman despise him."

Robert Eaves was a tall, slack jawed oaf with an effeminate manner and an inclination to sarcasm and insult. He needed particulars from me for the crew list he was typing and summoned me to the radio room. In an imperious, arrogant manner he asked how many dependents I had. When I told him his upper lip curled, " I suppose you've never heard of birth control. It's people like you who are over populating the world." This charming utterance from a man of uncertain gender, and a stranger to boot, rendered me temporarily speechless.

I suppose a good punch in the face might have changed his attitude, but from past experience I knew that I might get the worst of it, besides I had just joined the ship. "You are an ignorant buffoon" I said weakly, unable to think of a biting answer to such a remark. As is so often the case, one cannot think of a good retort to an insult until afterwards when it is too late. Eaves was a man to be avoided and I never spoke to him again. Although I did overhear him tell one of the engineers, that when he went ashore in Corpus Christ, he always spent at least $20 on books. He refused to pass them on to others, saying " If other people are too tight-fisted to buy their own books, I'm dammed if I will share mine, so I throw them over the side." Fortunately, Eaves left the ship a month after my arrival and was replaced by a West Indian, Sparks, who was easy to get along with.

34

Mirageone, Haiti

Once the cargo was unloaded we sailed for Miragoane, Haiti. I looked forward to seeing something of this country which occupies the western third of Hispaniola. The notorious, mad dictator Papa Doc Duvalier had died a few years earlier. He had dabbled in black magic and made political decisions after inspecting the entrails of dead chickens. Now his imbecile son, Baby Doc, was in power and according to reports, was no better than his father.

Although predominantly Catholic, Haitians still followed West African cultural practices. It was common to see a statue of the Virgin Mary standing among flowers in a shrine on the side the road, and beside it a stuffed figure with pins stuck in it. A strange mixture of Catholicism and Voodooism.

The master of one of the Caribbean Steamship Company's ships told me about a seaman who lost the will to live, a victim of witchcraft. " We were Northbound en route for Corpus Christi when the steward reported to me that one of the engine room ratings was very sick, a Haitian called Cyr. The steward, being in charge of the medicine chest, was unable to find anything wrong with Cyr. His face was expressionless, eyes glazed, staring into space. Stories about Cyr had circulated among the crew; it was said the his wife in Mirageone had seen the local witch doctor and that a collection of pierced dolls and headless chickens were seen outside Cyr's house."

"On arrival at Corpus Christi I notified the company and Cyr was taken to one of the best hospitals in Texas. He was put on a special diet, given every conceivable test, but despite this he began to lose weight. After ten days the doctors said that they could find nothing physically wrong with Cyr; he had simply lost the will to live. We took him back to Haiti, and on the way there he was put in the passenger accommodation, isolated from the rest of the crew who wanted nothing to do with him. In Mirageone he went to stay with the Catholic priest, and he was shunned ashore, as he had been aboard ship. He continued to lose weight and was now only 150 lbs; he had been a strongly built man of 200lb and in his prime. A week after we landed him, he died."

Haiti had the lowest standard of living in the Western Hemisphere, with an annual per capita income of less than $100. It was said that the prostitutes who hung around the dock area, could make more money in one night than a labourer could earn in one year. Another source of income for desperatly poor Haitians was the sale of plasma to the U.S.A. blood banks. A man or woman could make a dollar or two for being a donor. It was known as "Blood money." Baseballs were made in Haiti. These items, plus bauxite were among the few commodities for export.

The town of Mirageone (about 70 miles west of the capital Port-au-Prince), was a cluster of tin-roofed shacks amid a few substantial red-bricked buildings. Amidst these, the white- painted steeple of the catholic church rose in triumph. From a distance the country appeared deceptively tranquil, but a trip ashore revealed it's real character; one of oppression and poverty equal to the worst destitution I had seen anywhere.

The black Haitians, descendents of African slaves, lived an impoverished existence. They represented 95% of the population who barely eked out a living, while the other 5% were the mulattoes. They were the ruling class who lived in air-conditioned mansions up in the hills, well concealed and removed from the masses. Whenever resentment among the oppressed showed signs of turning into rebellion, the bogeymen or Tonton Macout, sadistic enforcers of the military regime, went into action with savage brutality. Bodies were left lying in the streets as a chilling reminder to would-be dissidents. Many people simply disappeared. This mayhem occurred in a country only a few hundred miles from the United States.

The pilot skillfully turned the ship in Mirageone Harbour in order to put her alongside the bauxite dock, with her bows facing seaward for an easy departure. This was no mean feat in such a confined space, with rocks so close at hand. At dusk it was cool enough to go ashore. Manfred, the German 2nd engineer, had asked me for a favour. He needed a case of 3 star rum and since I had enjoyed a few beers in his room, I felt obliged to return his generosity.

A rough, unpaved road followed the shoreline to the town about a mile away. The area around the dock was well lit but there were no electric lights along the road, and the shacks on either side were only dimly lit by flickering oil lamps. At first I felt apprehensive as I entered the outskirts of Mirageone. People came out of their shacks to inspect the stranger in their midst and called out in their patois, and receiving no reply, there was laughter and friendly inquiries. "Hello mister, what you like?" or "You got cigarette?" It was not menacing chatter, merely voices reaching out in a friendly way so I called out, "hello" in return, wishing that I had tobacco to hand out.

In the road to Mirageone, Haiti

I stopped outside one shack where a family were gathered around a table. Little children giggled and shyly covered their faces. The light was so poor I was only able to see their faces when a few feet away. I walked on with confidence, there was nothing to fear from these unfortunate people. The bogeymen were another matter. They lurked about in the shadows dressed in khaki, wearing dark glasses and armed to the teeth.

In the centre of the town the surface of the main street was rough, hardened mud; there were no sidewalks. The street was crowded with people shopping for meagre supplies of food and other basic requirements of life; clothing, pots, pans, and crude pieces of furniture. One stall sold bars of unwrapped red soap; it reminded me of the rough carbolic soap issued aboard tramp ships, but possibly better than the perfumed, fancy variety for sale in the shops at home. Whatever shortages there were of necessities, rum was in good supply, and for a few notes of rumpled currency I purchased a case of six bottles. It was more weight than I cared to hump back to the ship.

I stumbled about on the rough road encumbered by the rum, and heard the chatter and laughter of women close behind. In the half darkness I saw that they were carrying large earthen pots on top of their heads. One called out " Where you go, mister? Come here, I love you, mister." These invitations were mixed with colourful entreaties which are better left unmentioned. Aware that they had certain designs on my person, I increased speed and was relieved to reach the ship with rum, and virtue, intact.

Before leaving any port in the West Indies the ship had to be searched for stowaways. We had just dropped the pilot off Miragoene, when one of the engineers discovered three Haitians hiding in the steering compartment. The pilot boat was recalled and the men were sent ashore. Captain Mc Coy was furious and quite understandably vented his anger on me. I had made a hurried search, but on a ship the size of the *Richard* it wasn't possible to do a thorough job without delaying our departure. The master would have been in serious trouble with the U.S Immigration Authorities, and the company, if the stowaways had been aboard when we reached Corpus Christi.

This episode brings to mind the experience of a friend, Captain Joe Marston. In 1936 Joe was an able seaman aboard a British tramp which sailed from a port on the Pacific coast of Panama with a load of bananas for the West Coast of the U.S. She had been at sea for four hours when three stowaways were discovered hiding in a lifeboat. The Master was a hardcase Glaswegian who had no intention of keeping freeloaders aboard and was averse to wasting time by returning to port. The ship was turned about and steamed towards the coast. When a mile or so off the beach the ship was stopped, the stowaways were given lifejackets and ordered into a life boat. Seamen lowered the boat over the side and it was rowed to a point short of the surf, where the stowaways were pushed over the side. While they struggled ashore onto the deserted beach the lifeboat returned to the ship and she steamed away.

The master must have felt some satisfaction on having solved a thorny problem, but he was in for a surprise. A few weeks later, the ship, bound for the U.K., arrived off the Pacific side of the Panama Canal and dropped the anchor. The agent came aboard with a message which requested the master's presence ashore to attend to important business. As soon as he stepped out of the launch onto the dock he was arrested by Panamian Police and thrown in jail.

The authorities had not taken kindly to his treatment of the Panamanian stowaways. Meanwhile aboard the ship, the first mate took command, the 2nd and 3rd mate moved up the ladder and because Joe Marston had a ticket, he got his first job as 3rd mate. He was delighted to get this unexpected promotion. Alas, it was short lived. While the ship was passing through the canal, the British Consul in Balboa was busy trying to bail the master out of jail. This he did, but it seems that the judge absconded with the bail money and the case collapsed. The master returned to take command of his ship anchored off Christobal. Joe packed up his belongings and returned to the fo'c's'le, after holding a third mates job for only 12 hours.

Among the Richard's complement were a gang of American workers whose job it was to do repair work at sea. This was something I had never seen before aboard British, Canadian or American ships. The Richard was registered in Monrovia and flew the Liberian ensign, (a flag of convenience), and the owners were anxious to cut the cost of their ships lying idle in port undergoing repairs. The repair men were only aboard when the ship was in ballast and the holds empty. Badly corroded sections of steel were removed by cutting torches and new pieces welded on; thus on the run south, sand blasting and repair work went on continuously.

Another example of resourcefulness was evident in Mirageone when the engineers wanted to re-pack the stern gland. The chief engineer asked the mate to lift the ship's stern out of the water. Zeljko, the mate, obliged by directing the first load of bauxite into No.1 hold. This had the desired effect, the bow went down, the stern lifted up and the engineers did the job in a few hours, thus saving the company the expense of drydocking.

The Chief Engineer wanted the stern lifted clear of the water, and the mate obliged

On Christmas Day 1972, I wrote a letter to my daughter Bernadette:

" During my afternoon watch we were off the Cayman Islands. The Jamaican quatermaster and I were by ourselves on the bridge while the other officers and crew were celebrating Christmas, 300 feet away in the after end of the ship. One of the seamen must have thought that we were hungry when he came to the bridge with plates of chicken, prawns and pieces of steak. The quartermaster was able to eat his food and still steer the ship, while I only ate half of mine and threw the rest overboard. There were no seagulls in sight, and the lone frigate bird wasn't interested"

"Christmas dinner was at 5pm. It was a lavish affair. I have never seen a shipping company putting out so much food and an unlimited amount of alcohol too. A sign on the table read "Drinks on the house." With this sort of largesse surely they don't expect men to go on watch completely sober. It bothers me to consider the abundance of food we have when only a few days ago we were among the people of

141

Haiti who have so little. We were in Mirageone and I sat down to a meal of steak, and less than a mile away there were hungry people. But I cannot go ashore and give food away because the more aggressive beggars would take it from me before I reached the really needy."

35

Corpus Christi

In Corpus Christi there were certain hazards ashore for those seamen careless enough to carry large sums of cash in their pockets. The agreement which the West Indian crew had with the company stipulated that after a year's work, they were entitled to two months leave. This seemed rather unfair, when the officers only had to work for six months to get the same time off. On completion of a year's work, a man would be paid -off and after packing his bags would take a taxi to take him to the airport. On some occasions the taxi driver would bring along an accomplice, the unwary seaman would sit in the back, and when the taxi reached a deserted area a mile or two down the road, the driver would stop and produce a gun. He would relieve the seaman of his year's earnings, order him out of the taxi and drive away.

Parts of Corpus Christi were dangerous too. Willy, the Haitian officer's steward, had gone ashore looking for what he called "A good time." He left with a fistful of dollars and a few hours later came back with empty pockets and looking the worst for wear. He wasn't drunk, he had been beaten up. Entering a tavern in the rough section of town he met a girl who offered to take him home. He agreed and left with her. She was a decoy for a couple of thugs who roughed him up as he left the bar and then robbed him. By curious coincidence the police arrived on the scene, arrested the thieves and retrieved the money. Willy was bundled into the back of the police car and questioned. The police gave him enough money for a taxi back to the ship, but kept the rest!

Bank robberies were evidently a frequent occurrence. One afternoon I happened to alight from the company bus in the centre of Corpus Christi, as sirens wailed and several police cars arrived. The men in blue with guns drawn, rushed toward the entrance of a nearby bank but no shots were heard, and I wondered whether the desperadoes were caught.

The 'Knockdown' boys

I was aghast at the wretched conditions in which the crew worked during the unloading of our cargo. Zeljko, the mate, sent me down into the hold to investigate a delay in the flow of cargo ashore. The bauxite dropped from hoppers at the bottom of the holds, on to the conveyor belts and this flow was controlled by seamen stationed in the conveyor deck, who turned valves on commands bellowed from loudspeakers. These orders came from the foreman sitting in his control hut high on the stern who had the responsibility (under the mate's supervision), to ensure that the cargo was discharged properly. Because some of the bauxite stuck on the sides of the chutes, seamen, armed with shovels and crow bars were sent to clear it. They were called the "knock down crew."

I climbed down the ladder into the conveyor belt deck where the heat was overpowering, and the noise of the machines driving the belts only added to the hell below decks. Visibility was restricted to a few feet so I felt my way gingerly along a narrow platform, which led between the whirring conveyor belts only inches away from my head. Seamen, their faces covered to keep out the dust, eyes only showing worked at the valves; phantom-like figures in the swirling dust. Communications were only possible by sign language and by shouting into a man's ear at close range. I discovered that two men had been forced to leave their posts for good reason. One man said that he had a severe toothache, and the other complained of dizziness and wanted to see a doctor. The fact was the men hated "knock down" work and I understood why.

After half an hour in thi4s hell I was glad to go up on deck to breath fresh air. On explaining to the exasperated mate the reason for the delay, he delivered the classic line, "Anton, It is nothing but goddammed fuckery. These 'knock down' boys are no good knockers."

On hearing this I burst into laughter, Zeljko looked puzzled, "Anton, why you laugh? It is not funny."

" You're right it isn't, but its the way you say it, Zeljko."

I needed time for a smoke, and to reflect on Zeljko's memorable utterance. I retreated to a more peaceful area of the ship.

During meal breaks Zeljko occasionally made furtive trips ashore to a shack near the dock gate, where a woman called Amanda sold fruit. "My dear Anton, be a good fellow and watch the deck for me. I have important business ashore. Be back soon." He wasn't interested in buying bananas or oranges, there were plenty of those aboard ship. Behind the curtain at the back of Amanda's stall was a bed, on which she conducted her real business. Zeljko returned with a wide grin on his face. " Anton, it is good for my body, and I think it helps my head too."

37

En route to Scotland

Early in 1973 we were back in Jamaica. Instead of loading bauxite in Ocho Rios we went to Alligator Pond Bay, on the south coast, to load 45,000 tons of alumina oxide. This white powdery ore is the substance resulting from processing bauxite before the production of aluminium. I was delighted to hear that we were bound for the British Aluminum plant in Invergordon, Scotland. A new master came aboard. Captain Polderman was a hard to please, aloof, moody man who had spent most of his seafaring life on the coast of Surinam,(formerly Dutch Guiana).

My first brush with Captain Polderman came when I was on watch and we met another of the company's ships heading in the opposite direction. I had been talking on the R/T with my counterpart in the approaching ship. We had exchanged information about matters of mutual interest. When we drew abeam, one mile apart, he blew one blast on his whistle and I replied with one blast on ours. This brought Captain Polderman bounding into the wheelhouse. "You stupid man. Don't you know the proper signal when we meet a company ship?"

"Never heard of such a signal." I said irritably, stung by his insulting manner. "To the best of my knowledge it is not in the Rules of the Road."

The captain was not satisfied with my reply and mumbled something about my lack of professional etiquette. I felt uneasy after this encounter. It didn't bode well for the future. I consoled myself with the knowledge however, that in a few more weeks my term of service would be up, and I would go home.

We steamed north through the Windward Passage, and I was on watch in the early hours when we entered the Crooked Island Passage. While busy taking bearings to fix our position I noticed a large passenger ship on our starboard quarter; she was a blaze of lights and overtaking us rapidly. I decided to talk to her. Gone were the days of using a lamp to send messages by morse code. This had been replaced by radio telephone and it made communication simple. I picked up the microphone. "This is the bulkship *Richard* in the Crooked Island Passage, calling the ship on my starboard side." I was pleased to get an instant reply. "This is the Q.E.2. bound for New York." replied the Scottish senior 2nd Officer. I asked him why she was in such a hurry, as cruise ships usually steam at moderate speeds. " We are doing 29 knots to make up for lost time. Good night and Bon Voyage." The huge liner swept past us and was soon out of sight.

Ten days later we were approaching the coast of England. The usual route for ships from the West Indies bound for Cromarty Firth was up the West Coast of Scotland and through the Pentland Firth. The *old man* would have preferred this in order to avoid heavy traffic in the Channel and Straits of Dover, but we were ordered to refuel in Falmouth and thus we had to take the latter route. The captain seemed apprehensive when he asked me whether I was familiar with the Straits of Dover. I told him that although I had not been in those waters for twenty years, I was confident that we would have no trouble, as long as there was no fog.

38

The Straits of Dover

From Falmouth we headed up the English Channel and were off St Catherines Point before sunset. The book dealing with the rules of separation of traffic in the Straits of Dover lay on the chart room table; it stated that north bound ships must keep to the starboard side of the Straits. I heard the old man talking to the mate about this and as he preferred to plot the courses himself, I assumed that this was the route he intended to take.

When I arrived on the bridge at midnight I expected to find the ship on the French side of the Straits. To my surprise we were steaming off the white cliffs of England on the wrong side of the channel. The next four hours were among the most frantic I have ever spent on the bridge of a ship at sea. On the radar screen I counted over fifty ships ahead of us.

I expected the captain to deal with the navigation in such crowded waters, but he seemed content to watch me sort out the myriad red, green and white lights which appeared on both bows. He remarked on the density of traffic and I felt like telling him that our dilemma could have been avoided if he had followed the separation rules. I merely observed that we were now in the busiest waterway in the world. We had not only oncoming traffic to deal with, but channel ferries crossing our bow.

Close quarter situations became inevitable with so little room to manoeuvre. We were steaming in the wrong side of the channel at 16 knots into unfriendly traffic, and I could well imagine what the masters and mates were saying in the wheelhouses of small coasters as they streamed past us. Some were so close that I could see faces peering out of the windows. No doubt such exclamations as "Those ignorant bastards are on the wrong side," were being shouted in our direction. I felt sympathy for them but not for long, we had to look out for ourselves in this predicament.

I became concerned when a bright flashing light appeared ahead and a quick look at the chart showed no such light. Aware that our charts of this area had not been kept up to date, I rushed into the chartroom and was relieved to find a current copy of Brown's Nautical Almanac on the book rack. A hurried consultation revealed that the light ahead was the South Goodwin beacon, and we needed to alter course immediately. This light marked the southern extremity of the dreaded Goodwin Sands. Ships that piled up there seldom got off.

We weaved our errant way north, edging round the sterns of ferries, coming far closer to oncoming ships than we would in open waters. A blaze of lights dead ahead only added to my apprehension. It was a vessel engaged in some kind of underwater work and a wide berth was required. We arrived off Deal shortly before I went off watch at four; the traffic had thinned out by then. I had posted a letter in Falmouth to my uncle who lived in a house overlooking the sea. I told him that when the *Richard* was off Deal I would flash a light in his direction, but it was now 4 am and I made no signal, knowing that he would be in bed. Soon we were in the open waters of the North Sea. It was a great relief when the mate appeared on the bridge, and I went below for some much needed rest.

39

Bound for Halifax.

Our stay in Invergordon was brief, as the discharge of alumina took less than three days, but I did have time to go ashore and do a favour for the mate of another of the company's ships. He came aboard before we left Corpus Christi and had asked me to deliver his sextant to his home in Inverness. The train traveled at a leisurely pace through scenic, lonely country and finally reached the capital of the Highlands at the top of Loch Ness. Once I had delivered the sextant it seemed a waste to hurry back to the ship without taking a look at the city. I wasn't disappointed, and after a good dinner decided to spend the night in the station hotel in order to make an early departure next morning. It was worth the expenditure of hard earned money to sleep in a very comfortable bed for a change, and I returned to the ship a few minutes before my watch at noon.

I expected an uncomfortable trip across the Western Ocean in winter and even with 10,000 tons of water ballast, once clear of the Pentland Firth we began to heave about in heavy seas. We were bound for Halifax, Canada to pick up a load of Gypsum for Jacksonville, Florida. The weather became progressively worse as we headed west. The officers' accommodation was in the stern, and when the ship lifted her propeller out of the water the vibration made life uncomfortable.

One night, after bracing myself in my bunk in such a way to prevent falling out, a particularly heavy sea threw the ship over and I was thrown onto the deck, followed by my mattress. I spent the remaining few hours sleeping on the deck. When it was time to go on watch, instead of taking the usual route to the bridge via the main deck and risk being soaked, or worse, I went down to the safety of the conveyor belt deck and walked forward in total darkness. It was an eerie feeling as the ship pitched and rolled heavily, and I felt trapped inside an enormous cavern pounded by raging seas from without.

Our great circle track across the Atlantic took us into high latitudes, and we made landfall off the coast of Labrador and found ourselves in pancake ice for a day, before reaching warmer waters. After nine days of punishment we tied up in Halifax. Our stay was brief, but as the

The 'Richard' in pancake ice off Labrador

gyproc thundered aboard through large spouts into our holds at the rate of two thousands of tons an hour, I had the pleasure of a visit from my eldest son Andrew, and his girlfriend Mary. Considering the conditions in which I was living, I wondered whether he was glad that he was pursuing a different career.

40

Back on the Bauxite Run

The first two days of the trip south to Jacksonville was in the teeth of storm force winds. I stood on the stern looking forward and was able to see how the ship bent when lifted onto the crest of a sea. Later, when we were about 200 miles off the coast, I was on watch at night when I sighted many lights appeared ahead. It was a Spanish fishing fleet and I had some anxious moments finding a clear passage through it.

We discharged our cargo at a dock about 10 miles down river from Jacksonville. I wanted to see the city and persuaded the agent to give me a lift to town. It had been thirty years since I last walked the streets of Jacksonville. I had happy wartime memories of a three month visit in 1943 when the tanker *Murena* was in drydock, and the crew had enjoyed the hospitality of war time Jacksonville. But it had changed, and not for the better. Recent race riots had left ugly scars.

The once elegant Mayflower and Rooseveldt Hotels, in which we had enjoyed carefree parties and romantic interludes, had fallen on hard times. They looked tawdry and deserted, with boarded up windows and broken stonework; they appeared ready for demolition. It was a depressing sight and after less than an hour in the city I found a bus whose route took me a mile from the dock. As I walked across scrub land toward the dock I reflected on the fact that nostalgic trips into the past seldom live up to one's expectations.

En route to Haiti I wrote the following letter:

20th Feb. 1973.
Dear Bernie,

"There are times when I wonder whether I will complete my remaining three months of contract with the company. The problem

153

is, I have difficulty getting along with the captain. I had been on my feet for 15 hours as we discharged 35,000 tons of gyproc in Jacksonville. Exhausting work .The hard part was the continual climbing up and down the ladders into the holds. I have to fight fatigue. A coffee and a smoke, every now and then, gives me an extra bit of pep. I was hoping to be relieved by another mate so I could have breakfast, instead the captain came on deck and began to complain about something. He had spent 8 hours in his bunk, which was his prerogative but instead of helping us, he seems to want to hinder the loading of the ship.

The Yugoslavs and West Indians detest him because of his overbearing manner. It appears that he is one of three captains in the company who are very unpopular, and seamen will try to avoid sailing with them. Another master, by the name of San Sin, was so feared by the crew of the *Louise* (another bulkship), that life aboard was misery. The company heard about it and promoted him to a shore job in Trinidad, where no doubt he continues to raise hell among the natives.

After receiving another blast from the *old man* I decided to change tactics. In future I would adopt a more assertive attitude.

We were at sea and during the middle watch when the gyro compass suddenly ceased to function. This was not serious. The ship was being steered by auto pilot. I ordered the quartermaster to disengage the auto pilot and steer manually. I informed the captain, but he did not appreciate being woken, and began shouting, " Goddammit. Why did you call me? What's the matter with you? Do you have to tell me when the gyro compass stops?

Here was the chance to assert myself. I raised my voice to a level which I hoped, sounded more forceful "Yes Captain, I do. In the Standing Orders which you signed, the officer of the watch is instructed to notify the captain of any bridge equipment failure. That is what I have done." There was no reply. Why is it the some people look upon politeness as a sign of weakness? They only respect so called 'tough talk.'

See you in a month, or two. Love Dad."

154

41

The Chief of Police

My time aboard the *Richard* was coming to an end, and my last trip, was to Haiti. I wanted to go ashore to mail a letter to my father in England but didn't feel like walking a mile to Mirageone under a blazing hot sun. The chief of police was aboard for no other reason than to bum cigarettes from the crew. He wore the customary khaki uniform and dark glasses sported by the men in power in Haiti, and was a sinister figure. He looked like, and may very well have been, a bogeyman; one of Baby Doc's feared henchmen. On hearing that I wanted to go ashore, he volunteered to give me a lift on the back of his motorbike.

Unaware of any ulterior motives he might have, I accepted, naively believing that he only wanted to be friendly. We set off along the bumpy road in a cloud of dust and I clung on to the side of the saddle, bunched up against the chief. The butts of his pistols stuck in my ribs as we sped past the shanties, scattering peasants, dogs, cats and chickens, which lay in our path. It was a relief when we arrived intact outside the post office.

I got off the bike, thanked the chief and was about to walk away when he caught my arm." No, you give me cigarettes." His manner was threatening, his face had a steely look. I wondered how I was going to avoid trouble. "I will give you a packet later when I get back to ship." I said, pushing his hand away. " No, I want now." he raised his voice aggressively, "Not packet, you give me cartons. I want cartons of Lucky Strike." It was useless to argue with the chief of police, I was in his territory and I had visions of joining the list of missing persons.

"O.K. chief," I muttered nervously. "Two cartons it is. I don't have them now. I will give them to you next trip to Mirageone." To my intense relief he evidently believed me, and without further ado he jumped on his bike and sped off.

It was now past noon, the shutters on the post office door were closed; it was siesta time. Having made a special trip to mail letters, I was in no mood to give up. Despite having told the chief of police I would be back, I knew that this was my last trip to Haiti. I wanted to send Haitian stamps on a letter to my father, who was a keen philatelist. I knocked on the door and was surprised when it opened and a little old man led me into his musty, tumble-down office. He opened his desk and produced a large, dusty, brown book and began selecting stamps. The stamps were of low denomination and so many were required, it was necessary to stick some on the back of the envelope. I walked out onto a hot, almost deserted street and walked back to the ship. The letter never reached its destination.

Petar Stojpic, the Yugoslav 3rd mate, also had some dealings with the chief of police. He needed a Yugoslavian driving license which evidently was difficult to obtain at home, but in Haiti there was a thriving trade in illegal documents. The chief was able to provide him with a convincing licence on payment of an undisclosed fee.

In March 1973, my five months in the employ of the Caribbean S.S. Company was finished. I collected my wages, wished my shipmates good luck and went home. During the flight I had ample time to reflect upon the sort of life I had left, and felt fortunate to be returning to an easier way of earning money at sea.

42

The perfect job?

Within a month of returning from the West Indies I was standing on the bridge of the *Queen of New Westminster*. She was a 6000 gross tons, passenger and car ferry on the Mainland to Vancouver Island run. It was Spring of 1973; I was 2nd Mate and we were making the last trip of the day. In an hour I would be on my way home. In four days time I would have five days leave. This surely was the best sea job in the world.

Some seamen found the sailing back and forth between terminals tedious but I never found it so. The bridge watchkeeping was straight forward enough; keep clear of traffic and maintain the schedule. The main challenge for the mates and seamen occurred below, in the car decks, where they had to maneuvre as many cars, trucks and buses aboard, and possibly still sail on time. My preoccupation with this kept boredom at bay.

I had much to learn about packing the cars aboard without annoying the owners. Gone were the high handed methods employed in the old C.P.R. ships, when brute force was sometimes used to skid a card sideways into a space. Now cars were not to be touched. I hadn't been on the job for long before my zeal for cramming the cars aboard almost landed me in hot water. This happened because, in the process of persuading drivers to stop bumper to bumper, so close to the next lane of cars that some were unable to open the doors, they had to make the crossing imprisoned in their cars!

After a few months I was promoted to chief officer and transferred to Langdale, a terminal across the Howe Sound. The *Langdale Queen* was the oldest ship in the fleet. She was built early in the 20th century for the San Francisco Bay ferry service, but after numerous alterations over the years very little of the original ship was evident. The unique, solid brass, spokeless wheel was one feature which remained. Powered by G.M. diesels she had a good turn of speed, but her steering was woefully erratic and it took a good helmsman to control her, especially when approaching the dock. The master was a genial Scotsman by the name of John Kinnahan who made the job look easy. He was an expert ship handler, and in between terminals he would join me on the bridge to tell jokes and swap sea stories.

These were happy days. There were no crew troubles and the office didn't bother us. Some of the crew were entrepreneurs whose jobs in the ferries were secondary to their activities ashore. Bill Wiseman ran a thriving scrap business. Another seaman owned an apartment block. The 2nd Engineer was a farmer, and Bill Walker, a Master on another watch, was a property developer. Life ashore was pleasant for me too; I was a boarder in a house overlooking the sea, owned by a Mrs. Brown who worked in the ferries.

The house was a mile from the terminal, and after a few months I bought it. Two of my sons were frequent visitors as we set about improving the property. Andrew was living in Vancouver and Martin had managed to get a summer job in the ferries at Langdale. On my days off I went to Victoria to see how the rest of my family were getting on. In 1975 I was transferred to Victoria, getting a much desired permanent job as chief officer in one of the Victoria class ferries. It seems that I had finally made it; being in the right place at the right time. From then on I never looked back. It was plain sailing for ten years to retirement.

43

Setting the record straight

At first it appeared as if I had indeed landed the perfect job based in my home town, but there were clouds on the horizon, and this narrative would be incomplete if the following facts were omitted. The master of the *Queen of Esquimalt* was a tall, brooding man of few words and little wonder. A past mishap when his ship had run aground on a reef up the coast, had left its mark on him. Serious and enigmatic, one never knew what he was thinking. Evidently he was quite content to let me get on with the running of the deck department. Or was he? I was never quite sure.

A 'V' class ferry on the run between Vancouver Island and the mainland

The first indication that something was wrong came to light on my first day at work when the ship sailed from Swartz Bay, (the terminal near Victoria), bound for the mainland terminal at Tsawwassen. Once clear of the harbour the Master went to his room and seemed unaware of what was going on elsewhere in the deck department. I was on the car deck. We had a full load of cars, busses and trucks and I wandered along the deck to make sure all was well before going on deck to attend to paper work. I expected to see the seaman whose duty it was to patrol the car deck, but he was nowhere to be found. The most likely place where a fire would occur was in the engine room or on the car deck, and I could not leave until the seaman was found.

As I walked past the ship's baggage van I glanced in the window and saw him sitting down reading the paper. He was not in the least put out and remained seated when I opened the door. "What are you doing here?" I asked. " What's it look like, mate? I'm catching up on the news." This reply seemed to indicate that he objected to being disturbed. "How can you keep a watch on the car deck from here?" I asked, barely able to contain my frustration. "Oh, that's no problem," he replied, " I can see everything that goes on." " Is that so?" I said with ill-disguised contempt. "Well you can get out on deck, and if I see you in here again, you will be in trouble."

Sensing that there might be similar problems elsewhere I went up on deck. The usual routine for the seamen on leaving harbour was to wash down the outside decks, general cleaning, or any work that was required, but there was no sign of any action on deck. I went to their messroom and was astounded to see four men sitting at the table playing cards. This, in full view of any passenger who happened to look in the window. "How long has this been going on?" I asked. No one even bothered to look up, and I repeated the question. "How long has what been going on?" said one man with a smirk, hardly deigning to look up from the game. "Every one of you can get out on deck right now." I ordered.

There was a pause. "What for? All the work has been done." said another man. " You are the new mate and a real shit disturber too. We always play cards." Feeling the need to assert myself more forcibly I raised my voice a few decibels. "Yes, I am the new mate and I am about to disturb a lot more if you don't move." They went out on deck, mumbling to each other about new mates who didn't understand the job.

I thought about my last job and the seamen aboard the bulkship *Richard* who worked hard in often dangerous, dirty conditions for small wages. They saw their families only once a year, and yet went about their work cheerfully. Here, aboard the *Queen of Esquimalt*, men were well paid for easy work which they were unwilling to do. The deck crew had evidently fallen into a serious state of complacency. On the surface it did appear that everything was running smoothly and the prevailing attitude was that, as long as an accident didn't happen, why rock the boat?

All the seamen, but one, on my watch were men in their late fifties and early sixties. There were ex-naval petty officers who, on leaving the navy, had joined the B.C. Ferries in the early nineteen sixties, when the service first started. They were among a number who had brought their naval ways into the ferries to form a cozy arrangement aboard the ships, and do as little work as possible. I soon discovered that one or two were on the bottle. It wasn't easy to prove but I did tell one man that drinking aboard a cargo ship was one thing, but quite another when carrying passengers. As chief officer I would expect to be fired if caught the worse for wear, and he could expect the same result if he was drinking on watch.

When I reported these activities to the Master he merely shrugged his shoulders saying, "It's the first I've heard of it." There was no assurance from him that I was doing the right thing. But once started there was no giving up, and I continued to press the crew to do what they were being paid to do. During the next few weeks there was a dramatic change for the better. Two men asked for early retirement and two others were sent elsewhere. The one remaining seaman on the watch was joined by four young fellows who were willing and eager to work; from that time onwards there was peace.

In such a pleasant job time passed quickly and soon the Master decided I was fit to take his place when he went on leave. But first I had to be shown how to handle the ship without causing undue damage; this was known as being" familiarized." The main object of the exercise was to avoid knocking down docks. This was not always as easy as it might seem particularly for deep sea types like myself who were unaccustomed to manoevering large ships.

The Queen of Esquimalt had fixed propellers, which meant that when approaching a dock one had to maintain sufficient speed to steer the ship and then gauge the right time to put the engines in reverse if damage to the dock was to be avoided. The problem was that the engines could not be reversed until the rev counter showed that the screws were turning at no more than 100 revs. On my first day of familiarization, the Master having nerves of steel showed commendable restraint when I approached the dock at higher speed than recommended. I was then forced to pull the control lever astern before the revs had been reduced sufficiently. We hit the dock with a resounding thump just as an angry call was received from the Engineer to inform me that the brake bands on the shaft were smoking! The Master as enigmatic as ever, never said a word. "Never mind, I was only practicing" I assured the 2nd mate who was apt to be critical.

While my life afloat had now settled into one of pleasant tranquility, it was very different ashore. It was ironic that after a twenty year search having found the job which would enable me to be with my family, my marriage fell apart, and I left the house on Amphion Street. Over the next few years I led a somewhat nomadic existence living in a series of rented rooms, and apartments. Getting to work on time was difficult, as I didn't have a car and I was obliged to swallow my pride and ask other employees for a lift.

I needed to live closer to the ferry terminal and I found a place in Sidney, 3 miles away. It was owned by an odd character called Dickson who had turned his home into a boarding house. It had been a four bedroomed family house but now housed a dozen or more unhappy boarders. Beds were crammed into every available space, make-shift arrangements to make as much profit as possible. Some of the people, (Dickson liked to call them "guests"), slept on portable cots which were assembled on his command at bed time. A notice board bearing the house rules was placed on a wall. He ran the place like a concentration camp. On seeing all this I knew that my stay would be a brief one. The housework and cooking was done by Dickson's wife, a woman with a desperately sad look which never changed. She appeared to be resigned to a life of servitude under Dickson.

I arrived on the premises in time for supper and it was an eye opener. At 6pm sharp, everyone was seated at their places. Dickson sat at the head of the table while his wife dutifully placed the bowls of food before him. He then began to dole it out in meagre portions to be passed down the table. As a late arrival, I had been assigned a seat at the end of the table. The guests were mostly men and women of retirement age, although three or four men were much younger.

The astonishing thing was the silence. No one was supposed to talk until Dickson spoke. At first I thought I had landed among a religious

162

cult but the gist of what he talked about seemed far removed from the divine; he wanted to know why life was so unfair. He had worked his fingers to the bone to improve his lot but to no avail. There was something rotten about a world which had passed him by, but he would fight to change all this. Pointing at one of the guests a white-haired man who seemed more interested in feeding himself, Dickson asked for his opinion. " Jack, you should take more interest in what is going on around you. What do you think of the greedy politicians? You don't care, do you? Too damned lazy to do anything about it aren't you?" Poor old Jack muttered something about not wanting to get involved, it wasn't his business. Someone offered an opinion but was immediately shouted down by Dickson. By now I had heard enough. I finished my coffee, excused myself and walked out. Having been assigned to a cot in the basement beside the furnace I spent a sleepless night wondering how on earth I had landed in such circumstances.

Early next day I left to go to work knowing that I had to find somewhere else to live. I told the 2nd mate about Dickson and his strange household. "You should speak to Mrs. Karlsson." he said. "She works in the office and she usually has a room to rent." Mrs. Karlsson was a charming woman who would rent a room to me but not until the end of the month. I had to suffer five more days under the Dickson roof. In fact I spent as little time there as possible. On my last evening I took my place at the dining table. After Dickson had served the food and had begun talking in his usual brow-beating manner he turned his attention to me. "Where have you been? We haven't had the pleasure of your company for the past week." Sarcasm was one of Dicksons favourite weapons. "Don't you like the food? Perhaps it isn't good enough for you."

" No it isn't that at all." I said in a measured way. " I stayed away because I got tired of listening to the rubbish you talk. I find that it gives me acute indigestion. Perhaps this evening you will be good enough to spare us from your silly ramblings."

There was a moment of silence before Dickson was able to find his tongue, he looked rattled. " I don't like your attitude," he spluttered. "You can't speak to me like that in my house. I want you out of here right away."

As I was packing my bag in preparation for a speedy departure an elderly lady named Edie came up to me. " I have been here for over two years and you are the first person to stand up to him. I shook her hand, "Good bye Edie, you should not have to put up with his bullying. Get the others to help you, and together, go to Dickson and tell him that you will leave unless he changes his ways. Edie smiled. weakly. "I will try." she said. I spent a peaceful night at a motel in Sidney.

Problems arose with tenants in the house I still owned in Langdale on the mainland. Being an absentee landlord living in Victoria, a four hour journey away, meant that I was never sure whether the tenants were using the house in reasonable way or were bent on destroying it. Sadly it proved to be the latter. Andrew, my son and I made the long trip via two ferries to check on the premises to find out why the rent payments were not forthcoming.

We arrived unannounced and were surprised by what we found. We had originally rented the property to a young couple who appeared to be desirable tenants. However in our absence the tenants had invited half a dozen of his biker friends to move in. Andrew and I arrived at the door and were confronted by a pot bellied, bearded man in dirty jeans. A red bandana held a mop of hair away from his beady eyes. "Yeah. Who the hell are you?" he demanded. He became less aggressive after we identified ourselves but seemed reluctant to allow us inside the house.

We had heard complaints from neighbours about rowdy parties and of one drunken spree, when a horse was led into the basement for the amusement of the tenants, whose numbers had now risen to about a dozen. We were shocked on entering the once immaculate basement suite to find that it had been converted into a motorbike repair facility. Wheels, frames, tires and spare parts covered the walls and the once clean carpet was discoloured by oil stains.

Removing undesirable tenants was not easy, as the government at the time took the view that landlords were generally grasping and overbearing, while tenants were always the exploited ones. It took weeks to convince the ombudsman that our tenants were destroying the property. The matter wasn't resolved until the bikers suddenly decamped, owing a month's rent. I sold the place for less than I paid for it, and felt relieved to see the back of it.

Having proved myself as reasonably competent in handling ships, I was now able to relieve regular masters who had taken leave, or were sick. So in fact I spent almost as much time in command as I did as chief officer. But the real excitement took place below decks. As chief officer of the *Queen of Sidney*, on the run from the mainland to the Gulf Islands during the summer months, I was hard pressed to pack as many cars aboard and keep the master happy by enabling him to sail on time. This wasn't as simple as it was in the ships, which didn't call at places en route as we did. Carrying cars bound for three ports, I had to make sure that they were loaded in such a way that they were able to drive off in sequence. The general rule being; first aboard, last ashore. In order to achieve a good stow the last few cars had to be backed onto the ramp and into the car deck.

The master was an old friend, Captain Arnold Ryles. We had sailed together in the C.P.R. ships when I was a junior mate and he was a lowly Quartermaster. He was a good man to work with and there was ample time between stops to reminisce about the old days. One particularly busy day Arnie was curious about the method I was using to load the cars. I suggested that we change positions, he agreed and when we reached the dock and were about to take on a another load of cars, I went to the bridge and the captain went to the car deck. He was to supervise loading, a job he had done may times as chief officer.

After the last car had been loaded the master returned to the bridge. He appeared crestfallen. " What's wrong, Captain?" I enquired. He groaned " I can't believe it. The moment I go to the car deck some idiot drives his bloody camper into the car ramp. Smashed the top up, the silly bastard. I didn't even see it, just heard a mighty bang." "How's that possible, captain" I enquired smugly, knowing full well how such things occurred. " It all happened the second I turned my back on the incoming traffic. O.K. Tony, It's all yours now. Here's the name of the driver. He's fighting mad and ready to take you apart. I will take the ship out. You do whatever is necessary to keep the peace." I spent the next frantic half an hour trying to placate an angry passenger while filling out an accident report.

44

Captain Silas Backwater and others

The years went by pleasantly enough. There were occurrences which kept ship personnel from becoming too complacent through boredom. A certain chief officer (who shall remain nameless) had a propensity for jumping overboard while fully dressed in uniform, plus cap set at a jaunty angle. One summer's day, the *Queen of Victoria* was waiting for a berth at Tsawwassen and had stopped 2 miles out in the Gulf of Georgia. The captain decided it was a good opportunity to hold a emergency boat drill. It was also an opportune moment for the chief officer to inject some realism into the drill by consigning himself to the deep.

Having launched the emergency boat, the crew were straining at the oars when the chief officer suddenly abandoned the tiller, stood up and without further ado stepped overboard. The crew then rowed away, thinking that perhaps he had grown tired of his job and wanted to end it all. His anguished cries for help convinced them that he warranted recovery, and he was duly rescued. It was never established whether this odd behavior was a feeble attempt to draw attention to himself, to amuse the passengers, or to annoy the master. It happened more than once and the long suffering crew became adept at retrieving him from the sea. He would emerge from the depths, climb back on board with his entire ensemble dripping rivulets on the deck, squelch his way past gaping passengers who may have thought this stunt had been performed for their entertainment. Strange things happen at sea, even on ferries.

In 1983 a new ferry of the C. class joined the fleet and I was fortunate enough to be sent as chief officer for the inaugural run. The *Queen of Oak Bay* was a double ender of about 7000 grt and capable of 19 knots. Captain Mike Carter was in command and numerous dignitaries came aboard for the trip off the shores of Victoria. We were all surprised when the aged Captain Silas Backwater, retired commodore of the fleet, came aboard at the last moment. He appeared in full uniform and came to the bridge to give us the benefit of his wide experience. He enlivened the proceedings with a wealth of bawdy sea stories.

Captain Silas Backwater aboard the 'The Queen of Oak Bay'.

The following anecdotes are included in this narrative to show the reader a lighter side to life in the ferries:

The monotony of life in the wheelhouses of ferries was sometimes relieved by hearing lively exchanges over the radio telephone. One such conversation comes to mind when the master of the *Saltspring Queen* called the master of the *Pender Queen*. The former vessel was on the Swartz Bay to Saltspring Island run, while the latter was returning from Pender Island.

It was the practice to inform other vessels of the route a master intended to take on entering the harbour, in order to avoid a close quarters situation. The master of the *Pender Queen* intended to take the Canoe Rock route to Swartz Bay and made the call, " *Pender Queen, Pender Queen*, I am coming in by Canoe." There was a pause, then the reply, "*Saltspring Queen, Saltspring Queen*, You come in by canoe, I am coming in by ferry boat." There was no further conversation between them.

One of the smaller ferries was coming into Horseshoe Bay and was 10 feet from the dock when, to the astonishment of the crew, a man came running down the dock, jumped from the ramp and landed on the deck of the ferry. "What's the hurry?" said the surprised mate, "We are just coming in."

One of the large C class ships was coming into Horseshoe Bay.(Mode I = the aft screw only. Mode II = forward and aft screws engaged for manoeuvering and stopping ship)

Incident: Ship had smacked into the dock quite heavily, causing damage.

The quartermaster was Chinese- Canadian.

Interviewer at inquiry " What did you observe?"

Quartermaster " Cap.he turn ship into bay and line up the dock. Mate, he say to captain, You still in Mode 1, Cap." " Captain, he say " 'Clist'.

Interviewer : " Then what happened ?"

Quartermaster: "Ship hit dock with big bang- Cap. he say 'Clist' again."

Bunty Kapila, a former Bengal Pilot had just joined the *Queen of Prince Rupert* as chief officer. The master was Captain Jones, a genial, laid-back man whose previous chief officer was a quiet, competent Scot, who had blended well with the crew. The seamen, mostly ex-navy petty officers, seemed (to those of us who relieved on that watch) to do their own thing, led by the brazen George Hornett, the Union President. Bunty did not blend. He was ever conscious of his previous superior position, and this showed. As Captain Jones cleared the North Buoy, en route to Tsawwassen, he rang full away and began one of his much enjoyed yarns, the wheelhouse door was smartly swung open by Bunty, capped correctly, clipboard under left arm. No sooner had he reported to his master that the car decks were properly secured when the larger bulk of George Hornett was behind him, correcting him; there was somebody there boxed in, couldn't get out; it was the first vehicle on the starboard side. Bunty marched off to set his domain aright. When he saw the coffin-bearing hearse, he must have wished he was back on the Hoogli River.

45

Aboard the *Godfather*

In the summer of 1985 I became redundant (retired) and wondered what lay ahead. I didn't fancy the idea of retreating into a state of inactivity. The thought of finding a job at sea seemed attractive and when I was offered a skipper's job on a fishing vessel, I took it. The "Godfather" was a wooden vessel, 55 ft long with a beam of 16 ft, powered by a Caterpillar Diesel and speed of 10 knots. She had been built as a fishery patrol vessel, and was originally called the "Arrow Post." Her present owner had bought her for use as a fish buyer.

Our job was to follow the fleet of fishing boats and buy whatever they had caught. A sign above the wheelhouse said " Cash buyer" to inform the fleet that we were in business. We carried a crew of four. A buyer called Pat, he was a wild looking fellow with hair down to his shoulders and a mouthful of rotten teeth. But Pat was an experienced fisherman. Sam, the engineer and a deck hand by the name of Tom, and myself. Sam was the owner's brother; he was a big, bluff, sandy haired man who, as part owner of the "Godfather" had the most say, after consultation with the buyer, as to where we went. All I had to do was take the ship wherever they wanted to go.

I felt some concern before we set off from Ladysmith to join the fleet when Sam appeared at the door of my tiny cabin abaft the wheelhouse. He was holding a brown paper bag. "Hey Tony, I want you to sign for this cash."

"What cash?" I exclaimed suspiciously. Sam looked a trifle irritated by my apparent ignorance." This is the bloody cash we need to buy fish. There is $80,000 in here, and you must hide it in your room. Don't let anyone see where you have hidden it when you go to take out cash for a payment. There have been times when a cash buyer has been boarded at sea and robbed."

"Don't worry, Sam," I said airily. " It will be safe with me." I looked around my pokey cabin for a place of concealment and finally hid the bag underneath the mattress on my bunk

It was time to sail. As I gingerly handled the control lever for the first time, to manoeuvre the vessel clear of the dock, I suddenly remembered that I had neglected to count the money. But it was too late now. If I were a few thousand dollars short, who would believe me? Besides I had other things to think about. We were bound for Northern waters and because of the rush to join the fishing fleet I hadn't found the time to see whether we had all the charts we would need. The cash buyer monitored the fishing band on the radio to ascertain the whereabouts of the fleet and decided that we should join them in the Johnstone Straits, the body of water between the Mainland and Vancouver Island.

During the next few weeks we mingled with the fishermen and conducted business with them. I was kept busy manoeuvering among the boats, trying to avoid crossing over nets and making occasional trips to the hidden stash of cash to withdraw whatever amount was needed, and walking out of my cabin with a fistful of hundred dollar bills. I cannot remember keeping accounts; there wasn't time for such efficiency. These were arduous times, as the work went on almost non-stop with little sleep and the occasional trip to the nearest port to refuel and take on stores. I cannot pretend that I enjoyed myself, in fact I began to wonder why I had taken the job, particularly when I realized that there was little profit to be gained. This was because few fish were being caught and we spent a lot of time and consumed a lot of fuel chasing the fleet, only to find few customers.

But there was some excitement when we reached the Queen Charlotte Straits and the buyer received the news that a fishing fleet was out in the Queen Charlotte Sound about 20 miles away. It was vital that we should get there as quickly as possible so I chose the shortest route via the Goletas Channel. The weather was fine as we ran with the tide against a fresh northerly wind. Bob, the deck hand was at the wheel. He was a man who seldom spoke but on this occasion he yelled, "Skipper, What the hell is that ahead?"

I had noticed a strange sort of haze in the distance and picked up the binoculars for a closer look. About a mile ahead, the water appeared broken up and agitated; I looked at the chart and suddenly realized that we were heading for the dreaded Nawitti Bar. This underwater ridge covers an area no wider than half a mile, but because of the shallow water a dangerous rip tide occurs at certain stages of the tide. There was no point in turning around, I had to press on. With an ebb tide running against the wind we were in for a rough ride.

As we entered the turbulent waters the vessel picked up speed and within seconds her bow was lifting to short, steep seas. No sooner had we climbed over one wave when another came furiously at us, and broke over the bows; it was akin to riding a horse in a steeple chase. The old *Godfather* was shaken from keel to masthead as she reared up to face the onslaught of water, this punishment lasted for ten minutes until we cleared the bar and ran into calmer water. The wheel house door was flung open by a shaken engineer wanting to know what the hell I was doing with his ship. I do not recall my reply. There wasn't much I could say.

A week later with only a few tons of fish aboard, a closure was announced by the Fishery Department and we headed south to the cold storage plant on a barge at Sointula. After we had tied up, Sam told me that he needed parts for the diesel engine. After unloading the fish we went to Alert Bay, where there was a machine shop. As repairs would take some time, I decided to spend the night alongside the dock. It was a good opportunity for some of us to get a good night's rest but before turning in I wrote the following letter to my daughter Bernadette.

Aboard the *Godfather*. Alert Bay. 16th July 1987.

"My dear Bernie,

When I decided to join this vessel I thought it would prove to be an interesting and perhaps profitable experience. The events of the past few days have been a test of nerves. A lot of worry, and the kind of excitement I can do without. After several days following the fishing fleet, we had only 6 tons of salmon in the hold. The fishing had been poor so we decided to head south to the fish plant at Sointula, near Alert Bay, where we would unload the catch and go elsewhere in the hope of easier pickings.

We had only travelled a few miles when a radio message was received asking us to turn around and proceed to a boat which had a load of fish. He was thirty miles away but was unable to meet us en route

171

because his engine had broken down. After telling him that we were on our way, I discovered that I did not have a chart covering the narrow channel through which we would have to pass in order to reach him. I was in unfamiliar waters and it was now getting dark. Fortunately it was a clear moonlit night and even better our Nimkish Indian fish guide had knowledge of the route we were about to take. All went well. We found the fish boat, loaded his catch and after I had handed him a wad of money, I took the *Godfather* back through the channel. I almost hit the unlit buoy marking a rock at the entrance. This was a scare but more excitement lay ahead.

We now had about 7 tons of fish plus 30 tons of a mixture of ice and sea water in the hold, nearly 40 tons, so the vessel was deep in the water and down by the stern. As we made our way towards the open waters of the Queen Charlotte Sound we received a gale warning. At 0500 hrs we cleared the shelter of the land and headed out into the swells of the Pacific Ocean.

The old ship began to pitch and roll heavily. I had taken the precaution of making sure that everything movable was lashed down, and had added water into the hold to avoid the danger of a partly filled compartment. Now our stern was very deep. The motion became so violent that I thought it unwise to cross the sound in such a condition. With great care and judicious use of our forty year old engine, I turned the ship around and headed for shelter, which wasn't easy to find.

After a while I brought her to an anchorage close to the shore and we lay there waiting for the weather to improve. I then contemplated our next move. This ship is equipped with long pole- like masts which can be lowered to an angle of about 45 degrees and act as stabilizers. I decided to lower them and try to cross the Sound as soon as possible.

It was daylight when we set off out into the maelstrom and although she pitched heavily, the rolling was far less violent, and she was easier to steer. I expected to make the crossing in 5 hours. We had almost reached calmer water in the lee of the land to the west, when the young Indian lad who had come along to help, burst into the wheelhouse and asked for his lifejacket. I asked him why he needed it. 'Skipper, we are sinking! The stern is full of water!' I dashed out on deck for a quick look and glanced astern. Sam, the engineer, and Ben the fish grader, with buckets in hand, were baling out the flooded

172

lazarette (the compartment in the stern used for storing gear). We were now running with a heavy sea. Every now and then one would wash over the stern. I returned to the wheelhouse, reduced speed and considered sending a distress message.

Down by the stern after a rough crossing

I decided that we were in no immediate danger. We were two miles off Pine Island and would not have far to go if we had to abandon ship, although in a rough sea it would have been a difficult trip. Sam came to tell me that the pump was going full bore and the level of the water appeared to be going down. Soon we were in calm waters. I increased speed as much as it seemed safe to do so, and four hours later we reached Alert Bay. As soon as we were tied up I went on to the dock and looked at the *Godfather*. She was down by the stern at least two feet deeper than usual. The water in the lazarette covered several old mooring lines coiled below.

173

While the water was being pumped out and the lines brought on deck, I went ashore to purchase some oakum and two caulking irons. Possibly some recent rough weather had opened up the seams between the planking around the stern and they required recaulking. The deckhand and I spent the morning kneeling on a raft as we hammered the oakum in place. It did not entirely stem the inflow but reduced it to a trickle.

There are times when I wonder why I took this job, however there is some satisfaction in knowing that I can still cope in difficult situations, and afterwards I can usually laugh about it. Oddly it is the little things that bother me most; I miss not being able to have decent cup of tea first thing the morning. Now that the cook has left no one has volunteered to do the cooking and it is a matter of finding for oneself whatever food is available. There is eternal struggle to keep clean as conditions aboard are rather squalid. I look forward to a shower, room to move about, and a good night's rest in my soft bed at home. The thump and clatter of machinery is incessant and nerve wracking. Hopefully I will come out of this in one piece. Someday I will tell you more about it.

I look forward to seeing you. Love Dad"

46

Finding our way to Bellingham

As the takings became slimmer, we headed south and tied up at the dock at Ladysmith, near Nanaimo. I had a chance to go home for a few days and was considering other job opportunities when the owner called. He wanted me to take the *Godfather* to Bellingham, Washington to take on a load of ice, a requirement before making another trip to the fishing grounds. I told him that I needed charts for the U.S. waters south of the Canadian Border and he assured me that he would give them to his brother Sam, the engineer. Why it was necessary to travel so far for ice I do not know.

We left Ladysmith at dawn. An early start was essential as I had never been to Bellingham before and I wanted to arrive before nightfall. We were well out into the Gulf of Georgia when Sam came into the wheelhouse with a cup of coffee in his hand. " Good morning Tony, when will we get to Bellingham?"

"I have no idea but I will tell you when you give me the charts." I replied wondering why he was empty handed. " What charts?" he said gulping down a mouthful of coffee. Apprehension and anger gripped me. "Do you mean to tell me that your brother didn't give you the bloody charts I need to navigate in American waters?"

Sam wasn't the sort of man to engage in fruitless argument. "Don't worry, skipper, we'll get there." It was difficult to share his optimism. This was the first time I would be navigating without the benefit of a chart and in unfamiliar waters too. The Canadian chart only covered the waters to the International border and once we crossed into American waters, it would be a matter of guesswork. With no means of measuring the distance to Bellingham I had no idea when we would reach there if we were lucky enough to do so.

After passing the British Columbia Ferry terminal at Tsawwassen, I was in unfamiliar waters. But at least the weather was fine and clear. It was Saturday and several pleasure boats were nearby. I became anxious as we approached a narrow channel and decided to do what anyone would do when uncertain about their whereabouts; ask for directions.

A small boat, flying the stars and stripes, was stopped on our starboard bow, about half a mile away. A lone figure sat in the stern holding a fishing rod. I turned towards him, reduced speed and when within hailing distance, shouted, "Ahoy there. Can you help? I am bound for Bellingham and I have no chart, am I heading in the right direction?"

There was a long pause. Such an odd query may have flummoxed him. I asked again and this time I got a reply. He stood up and pointed in a southerly direction." Yeah, you are O.K. Just keep going until you come to the beacon on Vite Rock then turn left into Bellingham Bay. You can't miss it. Good luck."

An hour later I sighted the beacon my informant had indicated and after rounding a headland I sighted buildings ahead, which I assumed was Bellingham. It was, and my ordeal was almost over. A forest of masts appeared above the stone breakwater and I guessed that this must be the fish dock.

The entrance to the harbour was very narrow. A line of fish boats were inbound and an equal number were coming out. We joined the inbound throng and with heart thumping I managed to enter without incident. The harbour was chock a block with fish boats and I had to thread my way through this mass. Every dockside space was occupied, and to make matters more awkward I wasn't sure whether I was proceeding along the right channel.

As space became more restricted we bumped our way clumsily through the channel, receiving curses from boats owners angry at our rude intrusion. I was looking for the ice dock and no one we hailed seemed to care whether we found it or not. At last I spotted the sign "Ice" and with a huge sigh of relief I positioned the *Godfather* under the ice chute and she was secured.

I was anxious to go ashore in search of charts as our next port was Victoria which meant a long run in darkness through the Puget Sound, and there would be no room for guesswork. But it was Saturday afternoon and all the ship chandlers were closed. In desperation I went in search of the manager of the ice company and was lucky to find him, as he was about to get into his car. He was most obliging having sensed an urgency in my request and knew the owner of a supply store. Before long I was selecting two charts which would see us safely home.

When the invoice was made out for $28, I was embarrassed to discover that I had insufficient funds. A flash of inspiration told me where I could find the money, " I will be back in a moment." I gasped and bounded back aboard the *Godfather to* borrow the required amount from the brown paper bag under my mattress.

The 12 hour trip home was a relaxed and pleasant one. We arrived in the Inner Harbour of Victoria very early the next day. I packed up my belongings, locked the door of the cabin and walked the deserted streets to my home. I had considered borrowing the price of a taxi ride from the paper bag, but thought better of it. I haven't seen the *Godfather* since.

47

The *Beatriz of Bolivia.*

The notion of working aboard a luxury yacht is generally a very appealing proposition. I began to think about this, it would surely be more fun then chasing a fishing fleet. I bought a yachting magazine and an advertisement caught my eye. A master was required for a yacht in the South of France. This seemed to be just what I wanted as my daughter Bernadette, and her husband Scott were living in Paris; I could combine work with pleasure.

A phone call to the London yacht broker, who had placed the ad, revealed that the owner of the yacht was a Turkish millionaire who needed someone to take the place of the regular skipper, who had gone to Stuggart to improve his qualifications. I was bold enough to ask him whether my flight to France would be paid for. "No", he replied, "The owner will only pay your expenses from London. By the way, how old are you?" " Just reached sixty and feeling very fit." said I with conviction. "All right," he said," but the owner will want to interview you."

On reaching Paris I called Mr. Doryumglu the yacht owner. He suggested that I go to Antibes and look at his vessel, and if I wanted the job to meet him in Geneva.

I traveled south aboard the high speed T.G.V. and 12 hours later reached Antibes. Stepping out of the train into the wonderful warmth of an autumn evening on the Riviera, I wondered what lay ahead having arrived into a very different world of seafaring than I had previously known. After checking into a hotel I walked to the seafront and was astonished to see a huge collection of yachts of all shapes and sizes.

The so called mega yachts were in deeper water near the sea wall. There were ships almost 300 ft long. One, the 280ft *Nabila* owned by the arms king Koshnoggi carried a helicopter. Smaller ones lay in long rows, hundreds of them, with their sterns secured to the dock and an anchor holding the bow. This was known as a Mediterranean Moor. The yachts lay in marvellous precise order, spotless in every detail, their white and royal blue hulls glistening. Only very special and extremely costly paint would do for vessels of this calibre. Some of them had their names and ports of registry in gold embossed letters on their sterns.

Most of the yachts flew the British red ensign but would never enter a British port because they would have been subject to tax and marine regulations regarding certification. Many skippers held a yachtmaster's ticket, which for some vessels was considered insufficient. The yacht skippers were sometimes regarded with scorn by the men of the Merchant Marine, who referred to them as Mediterranean Cowboys. Yet with few exceptions these men were skilled in handling their splendid charges in very tight spaces, and took pride in their navigation and seamanship. Theirs was a specialized business.

There was the story about the retired master of a 300,000 ton super tanker. In recognition of his long service with the shipping company he was given command of their 100 ton yacht. He did not last long because he was unable to dock the vessel without damaging it and quit. Most of the yachts were motor powered but there were a number of elegant sail driven yachts with masts soaring high above the dock. I had never seen such a vast assembly of luxury afloat. It was claimed that there were about 2000 yachts in the marina in Antibes, the largest number in the Mediterranean. Many of them lay idle for months, even years on end. Others had to be in a state of readiness at the whim of their owners who might arrive on short notice with their families and a retinue of servants and they would expect to leave on a cruise immediately.

These were the kings, princes, sheiks, movie stars, newspaper barons and business moguls who liked to cruise among the Greek Islands or along the Italian Riviera. Some owners had no stomach for going to sea at all. They preferred to loll about in the sun at anchor off places like St Tropez and Cannes where there was more action, or merely remain in the marina at Antibes.

I set off to look at the *Beatriz of Bolivia* and wondered how long it would take to find her. I asked a bronzed sailor who was busy washing the decks of the lovely *Wanderer*. He pointed to an imposing building which stood high enough to overlook the great fleet, "Go to the port control office. They will know."

The Beatriz of Bolivia was moored nearby. She was indeed a fine looking yacht, but older than the larger and grander *Sheergold* which lay alongside her. I walked aboard and introduced myself to Fritz the Austrian engineer. "Ya Ya, so you are the new skipper. Well, you must take off your shoes too" he said with ill disguised disgust.

"Yes, of course" I replied apologetically (I had yet to realize that it was regarded as sacrilege to walk aboard a yacht without first removing one's shoes). It wasn't the sort of welcome I had hoped for but no matter. It didn't detract from the elation I felt on finding myself in command of such a sleek vessel.

The 'Beatriz of Bolivia' and the 'Sheergold',
in the yacht marina at Antibes.

The *Beatriz of Bolivia* was built in the early sixties by Camper Nicolson of Southampton. She was 125 ft long, her twin screws driven by Caterpillar diesels gave her a speed of 15 knots. My cabin abaft the wheelhouse was small, but comfortable with the convenience of toilet and shower. The owner's suite of rooms was luxurious; the walls of one of the owner's bathrooms was covered with hundreds of sea shells. There was accommodation for 15 guests. The *Beatriz of Bolivia* was worth $3 million and her annual berthing fee in the marina at Antibes cost her owner $110,000.

A year before I arrived in Antibes, a Greek tycoon, whose wife evidently did not wish to accompany him in his yacht, chartered the *Beatriz of Bolivia* for her use at a cost of $7,000 a day. She and her friends cruised among the Greek Islands for two weeks, then returned to Antibes. Months later someone reminded the Greek that the ship was still on charter. The bill for an idle yacht had run up to many thousands of dollars but evidently he didn't blink an eyelid at the extra expense incurred.

48

Fritz and the Terrible Turk

The seven hour rail trip to Switzerland for an interview with the owner, was pleasant, particularly as I felt free to charge Mr. Doryrumglu for my indulgence in the fine French cuisine aboard the train. I reached Geneva late in the evening and walked from the railway station along the elegant Avenue Mont Blanc, with a view of the lake on the other side of the city, and Alpine peaks beyond. I spent the night in the 5 star Hotel d'Alleves, which offered the sort of comfort only a man as rich as Mr. Doryrumglu could afford. The next morning after a good breakfast, I walked to an imposing building overlooking the lake. Mr. D's chauffeur ushered me into the conference room on the second floor and told me to wait.

A long table, with leather upholstered chairs, stood in the centre of the room. I stood for a few minutes looking at pictures on the wood panelled walls when the door opened and Mr. Doryrumglu walked briskly in. He wore a dark blue suit, was of average height, with short bristling hair, a stubby beard and piercing eyes. There were no formalities. He didn't say who he was, extend a hand of welcome, or ask me to take a seat. He got down to business immediately. " Why do you want this job?" he asked abruptly.

"Because I think it would be interesting." I said, feeling ill at ease and ill-prepared for this sort of interrogation. Mr. D stroked his beard and talked about the yachting community in Antibes. He despised them. "They have no morals, ethics, or integrity, they are thieves." "What do you think of Antibes?" I replied that I hadn't been there long enough to form an opinion. Mr. D became huffy " You will soon learn what sort of place it is. The French business people will cheat you. I want all receipts sent to me. Be careful, I want you to look after my yacht while the regular skipper is away. Are you good at accounting?"

"If you mean can I keep track of ships stores and the expense of repairs, yes, I have had experience in these things."

Mr. Doryrumglu looked irritable, and fired off another broadside. "What do you expect me to pay you?" I made a rapid calculation and remembered the skipper of the *Shergold* saying that he was paid 50,000 ff ($ 9000 U.S) a month. I couldn't expect to earn as much as that. "30,000 ff" I said optimistically. Mr. Doryrumglu grunted. "Send me your travel and hotel receipts." That was the end of the interview. He turned on his heels and left. Later the skipper of the *Sheergold* told me that I should have asked for twice as much and probably would have got it. So much for my business acumen.

Fritz and the skipper. 'Sheergold' in the background.

During my tenure as master of the *B of B* I tried hard to get along with the unsmiling engineer; to no avail. Fritz evidently didn't think I was fit to be in command of the yacht, which had been his home for a long time. My ways were too sloppy for his liking; he had the bloody nerve to chide me for neglecting to coil a mooring line in a yacht like fashion. Whenever I bumped into him I felt that he was about to click his heels, salute and stand to attention only to see me and change his mind. He seemed reluctant to answer my questions about the routine of life aboard, and replied in monosyllables as if he did not want an upstart, temporary skipper taking too much authority. I had the impression that he regarded himself as being in charge.

I hadn't come to Antibes to pick a fight with Fritz. Why spoil the fun? I would grin and bear it, I had little to lose. Anyway there were many other distractions in Antibes to keep me amused. Being a bit slow on the uptake I hadn't realized that I wasn't expected to do a stroke of work. All I was supposed to do was make an appearance dressed in white trousers, blue jersey and white shoes (supplied by the owner).

I was not accustomed to being idle aboard a ship. This was a very different world from the one I had come from. Alf, a Cockney from the East End of London soon put me right, "Skipper, relax and enjoy it while it lasts. The skippers down here have got it made. Some of them live ashore in luxurious villas; they come down to their yachts in the morning to look around, have a drink with the engineer, then they go ashore to play golf and that's all we see of them. Some men are away for weeks. They know that the owners don't care as long as their bloody toys are being kept up to snuff, and that's what we do."

Alf was a skilled carpenter and varnish man. "Anyone who can do varnish work can get a job here. Most of us are from England and English girls come here looking for a job. They ask me to show them how to varnish and if I have the time I teach them. It's a good trade, and it pays more than I could make in England for doing the same work. Which reminds me, the Turk hasn't paid me for over a month. He's as slow at paying us, as the second coming of Christ. All these bloody millionaires are the same. Getting your money from him is like extracting teeth."

Once the fact had sunk in that I was more or less free to do as I wished, I decided to spend more time ashore. It was most enjoyable to wander along the wharf admiring the yachts. Berthed close to the *Beatriz of Bolivia* was the sleek yacht, *Something Cool*, the aptly named 150 ft floating palace owned by Heineken the Dutch beer magnate. Ted, the skipper was an energetic Irishman who could usually be seen working fussily as he removed the slightest blemish on her gleaming hull. He was an expert in keeping it as smooth as glass.

Once a year Queen Juliana of Holland came aboard with her family and retinue and Ted would take them on a two week cruise. "It's the best job in the world", he said. He invited me aboard to sample one of the owner's products. I asked him whether he ever went home on leave. "Why would I do that?" he replied. "Working down here is more fun than going to Ireland, besides the weather is better."

Further along the dock lay the beautiful *Hussar* flying the flag of the United Arab Emirates. Her skipper had been a farmer in South Africa; "This beats working for a living." he said " I've been here six months and have yet to meet the owner. Nobody bothers me, but I have to keep her in top condition just in case he and his family turn up unexpectedly" The owner was an Arab sheik who always brought two cooks along with his retinue; one who cooked Arab food and the other catered to European palates.

I walked aboard the 200 ft *Vagabonder* and met the youthful Australian skipper, who seemed eager to show me some of the extraordinary refinements of luxury aboard his yacht.

She was undergoing a refit and a novel carpet had just been laid in the saloon; it emitted coloured lights due to the magic of fibre optics. At the press of a button wood panels slid aside to reveal television and stereo equipment. The skipper told me that when the Italian owner and his wife and children came aboard, he was treated as one the family. All they wanted was to be taken for a three week cruise along the Italian Riviera, and when that was over, he had the rest of the year to do as he wished.

In the wheelhouse of the *Beatriz of Bolivia* there was sophisticated equipment with which I was unfamiliar. It was vitally important to understand how to use the satellite navigation system in the event I had to take the ship to sea. I made friends with my neighbour, the skipper of the *Sheergold*, (Jack Cameron a tall, sandy haired, congenial Scot). He invited me into his sumptuous cabin and offered me a drink.

There always seemed to be liquor aboard the yachts yet I never saw anyone the worse for it.

The magnificent 'Catarina', under the flag of St. Lucia

Jack was one of the skippers who, as Alf said, " Had it made." He opened the refrigerator and handed me a beer, "I couldn't wish for a better boss. Mr. Harris made his fortune selling carpets and bought the *Sheergold* for $8 million. She is a Fed -Ship built in Holland, the state of the art as they say. Mr. Harris comes down here once a year with his family and says, "Well Jack, where will you take us this time?" I can take the ship wherever I please. We usually cruise the Greek Islands for just a couple of weeks. They don't spend much time at sea because his wife gets sea sick, so then we return to the dock in Antibes and that's it for the year. You must excuse me. I have a golf appointment in half an hour. I will come aboard your yacht tomorrow and run through the sat-nav system with you."

I felt concern about the delicate business of taking the yacht out of the harbour for there was nobody to explain how it should be done. Fritz would have been pleased to show me, but he would be in the engineroom. All seamen know about the fundamentals of ship handling in confined waters and the need to make sure that no lines are hanging over the side, and that the anchors are clear and ready for use. As she was a twin screw ship it should have been fairly straight forward. But putting theory into practice isn't always easy.

Fritz must have read my mind when he said. " Skipper, I want to test the engines. When do you want to take her to sea?" "Any time you want" I replied, pretending to show that there was nothing to it. Fritz was a wily fellow. I got the impression that he wanted to see whether I was equal to the task of taking the ship out, and returning without mishap.

Quite an audience was on hand to watch my performance as it wasn't an every day occurrence. The skippers of the yachts on either side were anxious about scratched paintwork, or worse. As the anchor was aweigh, the engines put on stand by, the lines let go, I grasped the engine controls. I had bolstered my sagging confidence by reminding myself that I had handled ships ten times larger than the *Beatriz of Bolivia*. But it can be a tricky business manoevering a ship for the first time in a very confined space. Anxious not to apply too much power I moved the controls very carefully and was relieved to discover that the yacht was responsive to the helm and propeller movements.

As we proceeded past the line of yachts towards the harbour entrance I increased speed. Soon we were abeam of the breakwater and out into open waters. I was just beginning to enjoy the feel of being at sea in such a splendid vessel when Fritz called from the engine room. He sounded angry " I have problem. Go back to the dock." He was never very polite, now his tone seemed to imply that I had done something to cause the trouble. We returned very cautiously to our berth without incident or fanfare. Fritz never did explain what the problem was, and I didn't bother to ask. Whatever it was, he had plenty of time to fix it.

Although the ship's refrigerators and storerooms aboard the *B of B* contained food, we were not supposed to dip into it. We had to look after our own catering needs. This evidently didn't apply to wine, of which there was a good supply. Fritz assured me that the owner's policy was that we could help ourselves providing we didn't over indulge, or worse, sell it. As Fritz kept the key to this bonanza and was frugal in dispensing it there was never a problem.

The centre of town was a pleasant ten minutes walk past the rows of yacht, to the medieval wall and arch which led to the shops and cafes of old Antibes. The favourite haunt among the yachting fraternity was the Cafe de Paris. This was where all kinds of shady deals were made, favours asked, money exchanged, and rumours circulated. I avoided the place.

I hadn't been in Antibes long before I realized that my inability to speak French was a great disadvantage. Most of the yacht skippers were British, a few from Australia and New Zealand. They had made it their business to have a working knowledge of French and some were fluent which was vitally important when conducting business deals in France. When a yacht was laid up for her annual refit, the skipper had an opportunity to make a lot of money. Men in suits, carrying briefcases descended on the marina, parking their Mercedes, and Rolls Royces alongside the yachts that were due to go for a refit.

A great deal depended on the skippers ability to negotiate a contract with the dry dock, engine, and hull repair contractors, in order to get the best deal for himself. This may not necessarily have been in the owner's best interests, but the owners either didn't know or care. All they required was that their yachts were kept in good condition, and the manner in which this was achieved was entirely up to the skipper. Jack, the skipper of *Sheergold* told me that when he took her through a refit, he expected to make at least $50,000. The contractors, suppliers and miscellaneous businesses involved in the lucrative yacht repair business were equally well rewarded.

I had been aboard the *B of B* for two months when I decided to look for another yacht job. I had heard reports from men who had worked for Mr. Doryrumglu and found him difficult to please. One skipper had received a terrific barrage of insults from him, when he had innocently walked along deck on the starboard side, which Mr. D had decreed was out of bounds for any of the crew. It seems the skipper was unaware of this and so a shouting match ensued, in front of the owner's family, and the skipper lost his job. Other men had run afoul of the 'Terrible Turk' and his reputation soon spread around the marina, with the result that no one wanted to work for him. I began to realize why I had been given the job and hoped that I could leave before Mr. D. wanted to go on a cruise.

The *Beatriz of Bolivia* was a beautiful yacht, but she was over twenty years old and there were signs of deterioration; a bubble of rust the size of a dinner plate had formed on her hull. This had conveniently been ignored and covered with several coats of glossy paint. I ordered one of the varnish experts to remove the rust and re-paint the area. " We don't do that kind of job." he said. "I only do wood varnishing work. You will have to get an outside contractor." I took his advice and was in the process of talking to a contractor when Fritz got wind of it. "You can't do that work on the hull. The owner won't like it."

"Fritz, as skipper of this vessel I consider it my business to maintain this vessel. You look after the engines."

Fritz stamped his feet and wrung his hands. "You will see. Mr. Doryrumglu can make a lot of trouble for us." There was no point in arguing. As relieving skipper I knew my job was only temporary and that Fritz had more say as to how the vessel was run than I did. I forgot about the need to remove the rust blister.

Most of the yacht radios were tuned into Radio Monaco, the English language station, which transmitted weather broadcasts, pop music and information about jobs on yachts. There was no charge for a brief message over the airways, which gave my C.V. to any yacht owner looking for a skipper. The only response came from the skipper of the yacht *Rosarita*. He didn't offer me a job but invited me to visit him in Monaco.

The train ride from Antibes to Monaco was an enjoyable one. The track followed the coastline passing through Nice, Menton, and Villefranche and into the Principality of Monaco. I walked from the station, through the city and to the picturesque harbour, where I spotted the regal *Rosarita*, secured stern to the quay, her bow facing the sparkling, azure waters of the Mediterranean.

I pressed the button at the foot of the gangway and the response from a loud speaker on the stern gave me permission to come aboard. Leaving my shoes at the gangway, I walked along the pristine teak deck to the bridge where the skipper, James McPhee invited me into the wheelhouse, handed me a beer and asked me what I thought of the yachting world on the French Riviera. "Its quite different from the outside world of commercial shipping, isn't it?"

"I left the Union Castle Line after seven years with the company. Promotion was so slow and as 2nd mate on one of the mail boats and with a master's ticket, I had no chance of a master's job before I was fifty, so I quit. A friend suggested that I should look for a skipper's job in Antibes. Within a week of my arrival I got this job; that was three years ago. I earn twice as much as the average master in British ships, and have much more fun, no taxes and no worries." I was about to ask him whether he had a family when an attractive blonde walked in with a tray of sandwiches. "Meet Marylyn the purser. She is also my wife" said skipper Mcphee with a chuckle. "She keeps the accounts, does the cooking and I pay her well. Don't I dear?"

I told James about the *Beatriz of Bolivia* and the irascible Mr. D. He laughed. "You have been unlucky enough to be stuck with the wrong owner. Nobody wants to work for him. Look around, sooner or later you will find a job which suits you and once you get your foot in with the right crowd, you can't go wrong. Some of the skippers down here don't even have a ticket. The *Castaway* over there is an example"

James pointed at the elegant motor cruiser with raked bow and streamlined superstructure, lying at anchor in the harbour. " Her skipper was a deck hand just a year ago. He was a smart fellow who had never set foot aboard a ship in his life, but he learned how to varnish the woodwork and keep up the yacht's appearance. When the skipper took her out for a cruise he promoted the deck hand to mate. The owner was impressed. Before long the mate took over the skipper's job and now earns $10,000 a month."

After two months in Antibes I was becoming restless. When I heard that the regular skipper was returning to the *Beatriz of Bolivia* I looked forward to going home. However I had not yet received any money from Mr. Doryrumglu and was about to remind him when Fritz came up to my room, he looked very worried. "The owner is coming aboard tomorrow. We must be ready for him."

" That's good," I said. "Now I can expect to be paid. Then I can take off back to Canada."

A white Rolls Royce arrived at the gangway. Mr. Doryrumglu had come to see his yacht and I hoped he would pay me off. He was as brusque as before. "What do I owe you?" he said taking out his wallet. I told him and he handed me a wad of francs. "I hear that you wanted to do work on the hull. Well it does show interest, but we leave that to the shipyard. It doesn't look good repairing my yacht here in the marina."

Hans, the regular skipper came aboard the next day. " How did you get on with Mr. D.?" he asked. " I got the impression that he wasn't very pleased with me " I said as I packed my bag. Hans laughed, " He is never satisfied with anyone. I won't be here for long. I have a better job to go to in a months time, then Mr. D. can find someone else." I wished him luck and left for Canada via Paris and London.

49

The *Bermuda Star*

Early in the summer of 1989, an employment agency informed me that a 2nd mate was needed aboard a cruise ship in Montreal. Arriving at the airport I spotted a dapper fellow in a white suit holding a sign, which said *Bermuda Star*. I assumed that this was a one-man welcoming party for my benefit, in fact he was there to assist passengers who had flown in to take a cruise. I attached myself to the group and saved the cost of a taxi to the dock where the *Bermuda Star* was berthed.

She was a handsome ship of 23,000 tons, 615 ft. long and a beam of

The 'Bermuda Star'. Alongside the dock in Quebec City.

84 ft.; built in 1958 by the Ingalls Shipyard for the Moore McCormack Line as the *Argentina* for their South American Service. She was powered by steam turbines, and twin screws gave her a service speed of 19 knots. Her streamlined funnel was a dummy; smoke was dispelled

through pipes on the goal post mast at the after-end of the accommodation.

The 'Bermuda Star'. View looking astern.

In 1972 she was sold to the Holland America Line, renamed the *Veendam* and refitted for the cruise trade. In 1980 I was in Vancouver and walking along the road overlooking the pier where cruise ships docked and I stopped to admire the white hulled *Veendam*. Little did I realize then that one day, I would be working on this fine ship. She was sold to the Bahama Cruise Lines of New York and became the *Bermuda Star*, registered in Panama.

Montreal in the summer months is hot and humid and it was with some relief when I stepped off the gangway into the air-conditioned interior of the ship. I asked the Nicaraguan quartermaster whether the captain was aboard. "No," he said. "He is ashore. You must see Carol, she is the2nd purser." There was a line-up of men waiting to sign on the ship's articles and others who were going on leave and wanted their pay. No wonder that the over-worked Carol looked tired and irritable. She had to keep track of the wages and leave entitlements of a crew of 300 men and women.

I handed her my letter of introduction supplied by the marine superintendent. Fortunately she didn't ask me for my discharge book. Had she done so she might have noticed that I was not as youthful as I claimed to be. I had considered it expedient to roll back the clock 10 years in order to get the job. This would work well enough as long I kept my wits about me and didn't boast about my wartime adventures.

The crew was in a state of great activity as 750 passengers had just disembarked, and another full load were about to board for a cruise to ports on the Atlantic coasts of Canada and the U.S. I met the Staff Captain on the bridge, a tall, suntanned, fair haired and handsome man by the name of Roger De Sales. He shook my hand and asked "Do you have a uniform?" " No" I replied, " I wasn't told to bring one." " Then you must see the ship's tailor, he will fix you up." Within 24 hours the Philippino tailor had outfitted me with two pairs of white trousers, three made to measure shirts and a uniform cap. I had to wait until we reached Philadelphia before I was able to go ashore and buy a pair of white shoes, thus completing the ensemble.

Jacques, the chief officer was a sour character from Rimouski, Quebec, who made an unflattering comment on seeing that the new 2nd mate was almost twice his age. I chose to ignore it. Serge, the 3rd mate was more friendly. He was more concerned about making sure that I was familiar with the bridge equipment. Captain Krantz came to the bridge as we were about to sail. He was a flamboyant man with a gold chain around his neck and a lofty manner. His Mexican wife and young son were aboard and the buzz around the ship was that he was more occupied with the social life aboard, than the running of the ship. These duties he left entirely to the staff captain. I went back aft to my station on the stern, armed with a walkie-talkie, and soon we were heading down the river bound for Quebec City.

When I went on the bridge at midnight, we were out in the open waters of the Gulf of St Lawrence and approaching the Gaspe Passage; bound for Charlottetown, Prince Edward Island. On my watch were the quartermaster and a lookoutman, both seamen from Nicaragua. I felt a little apprehensive about being in charge of a ship with which I was unfamiliar. We were steaming at 17 knots in waters I had last sailed in during the war years. Manuel, the lookoutman, was eager to help with such things as the location of various bridge equipment. He had been aboard for a year, and in between fixing the ship's position and keeping the log up to date, I listened to him explaining the ship's routine.

Wheelhouse of the 'Bermuda Star'

At 10 a.m. the following day I was roused from a deep slumber by blasts on the ship's whistle announcing a boat drill. The passengers mustered at their respective boat stations and were given instructions on what to do in an emergency; this was simple and straight forward enough. It was followed by a crew muster and that didn't go so well. About a dozen men turned up at my boat station and after checking their names listed on the muster card, I pointed to one man and said, "What is the signal for abandon ship?" There was a long pause, during which the man in question looked blankly at me. Another man spoke up, "He doesn't speak English." "Then someone will have to translate the question." I said, wondering what I would hear next. The question was asked in Spanish, his reply was relayed to me, " He doesn't know!" Some cruise ship companies insisted that all of their seagoing personnel understood English, but aboard the *Bermuda Star* it appeared that there were many who could not. This revealed a communication problem which could have been serious in an emergency.

View of the fo'c's'le head of the 'Bermuda Star'.

People from 26 countries were among the crew. The engineer officers were German and Greek; the ratings, West Indian, the Pursers were American and European. Most of the stewards were from the Philippines, the seamen were from Nicaragua, the cooks and galley staff were Italian and the men who worked in the laundry were from India. The ship's casino, souvenir shops, photography business, and most of the entertainment was run by an outfit based in London and staffed by Britishers. The cruise director was a jaded New Yorker, who claimed to have been on the stage in his younger days, and gave the impression that his talents were being wasted on the passengers.

We entered the Delaware River at dawn. It was one of those calm, clear summer mornings when it was sheer pleasure to be on the bridge, to stand back and let the pilot do the work. I could enjoy scanning the shore with the binoculars as we steamed up the winding river. As we approached the dock in Philadelphia I noticed a sailing ship lying alongside our dock, and we tied up right astern of her. It was the old windjammer *Moshulu*. She had been towed across the Atlantic from Europe and was now waiting to be restored to her former glory. I had been reading about this fine ship in Eric Newby's "The Last Grain Race," and felt saddened when I went aboard and found her in a run down condition.

One of the advantages of being aboard a cruise ship was that we usually docked near the centre of the places we visited. In Philadelphia it was a very short walk from the ship to the main streets of this historic city. The worst time for passengers and crew in any cruise ship, was arrival day in port at the end of a cruise. When that happened to be New York on a hot and humid day it was bound to be sheer misery, and for me it was a test of mental and physical endurance. Passengers could not understand the delays in letting them ashore and often voiced their frustration.

This was the case when the *Bermuda Star* arrived at the pier in Manhattan and 750 passengers were clamouring to go ashore. I had the misfortune to be on duty at the gangway. I had been given explicit instructions not to allow anyone ashore until the ship had been cleared by the Customs and Immigration Authorities. "Who the hell are you to tell me I cannot go ashore?" demanded a well fed, red faced passenger. "I'm an American citizen and I have a plane to catch. Are you gonna pay my hotel bill if I miss it?"

"Well, sir," I said in hope of keeping the peace, "It is your government which insists that I keep all the passengers and crew aboard until we have clearance." It was useless to try and reason with such people, they couldn't be mollified.

We had docked at 8 a.m. and during the next eight hours, 750 passengers and their baggage had gone ashore. Many crew changes had taken place, the ship had been refueled, re-provisioned, and another full load of passengers came aboard. It was my job to make sure that no unauthorized persons came up the gangway. A steady stream of people went up and down the gangway and it was next to impossible to inspect cards and slips of paper each supposedly identifying the holder. In the midst of this frenzied activity a marriage ceremony was due to be held aboard. A hundred impatient guests pushed their way up the gangway past a steady steam of people wanting to go ashore. It was chaotic. There was a huge sigh of relief from the crew when at 4 p.m. the pilot boarded, and we put to sea.

'Bermuda Star'

50

Taking it easy in Newport, R.I.

Newport, Rhode Island was one of our ports of call. It was a well known haven for the rich and famous families of America, among them the Kennedy family had a house there. Newport harbour lies in a landlocked inlet up the Rhode Island Sound. We arrived on a bright, sunny, breezy morning and anchored about half a mile off-shore. Many weekend sailors were out in the bay testing their skills on the choppy waters.

Our passengers were chomping at the bit, eager to get ashore. They had eaten a good breakfast and needed to work up an appetite for the next feast. Two passenger tenders had been lowered into the water to take them ashore. These craft were diesel powered with twin screws and they carried about 100 persons. They were as old as the ship; heavy, slow, clumsy and, as I was soon to discover, not easy to handle. The passengers boarded the tenders from a platform at the side doors in the hull. The 1st mate, Jacques, was in charge of No.3 tender and he set off for the dock in Newport, but his tender broke down when he was less than half way to the dock.

I was on the bridge when Roger, the staff captain called me on the walkie-talkie. "Tony, lower No 4 tender, load your passengers and tow the mate's tender to the dock." There was no time to time to tell him that I had never handled a tender, and had no idea what the harbour of Newport looked like. It was hidden from view behind the land. I took a quick look at the chart to get some idea of the way in, and went down to the embarkation deck.

Once we were loaded, I pushed the engine control levers forward and discovered that the engine speeds were not equalized. This resulted in one propeller turning faster than the other which effected the steering and I had to offset this with the helm. I ran my tender alongside No 3 tender with less than consummate skill which was a pity, because Jacques was in a cantankerous mood, and now I had given him an excuse for making unkind comments about my evident lack of seamanship.

The seaman with me took a line from No3 tender, made it fast, and we headed for the road bridge which spans the entrance to the harbour. There was a narrow gap between the stone piers and we ran full tilt, with our tow towards it. When we were under the bridge, I glanced anxiously astern and to my horror I saw our tow take a sheer to starboard toward the bridge pier. By great good fortune it shaved the pier by inches. The passengers had now begun to take an interest in this dramatic turn of events, and a chorus of oohs and aahs was followed by the clacking of loose dentures biting the warm air. The Blue Rinse set and their partners were getting more excitement than they had paid for.

I had difficulty handling one of these tenders.

Realizing that I had made a mistake by allowing too much line out between us and the tow, I slowed down while the seaman shortened it. This done, I looked for the dock, and saw that in order to reach it, we had to make a 90 degree turn and then pass between the bows of a very large luxury yacht, (The *Octopusy* of James Bond movies), on one side, and the sterns of three equally sleek craft on the other. This was another tricky situation fraught with unpleasant consequences, especially when I had a tow to contend with. Just as we entered the space between the yachts the tow took another sheer to starboard. This was definitely not my day. Despite efforts to stop it, the tender bumped the stern of the aptly named *Take it Easy*, a yacht of some dignity. There was a rattling sound followed by a plop, as some expensive fitting fell into the drink. I was now concentrating on getting alongside the dock. I managed it in some style and flourish. Our tow had enough forward motion to do the same. Our passengers cheered, and one old fellow had the audacity to congratulate me.

A passenger tender about to leave for Newport, R.I.

It is easy to understand why the yachting fraternity in Newport resented this rude intrusion into their peaceful weekend retreat. The very sight of several vulgar looking, orange coloured cruise ship tenders in their midst, must have inflamed high passion among the well bred. While the passengers were ashore, I had time to report recent events to the staff captain. I was worried about the return journey, being anxious to avoid further close encounters.

After an hour ashore, the weary passengers came back to the tenders. I took the controls of tender No 4 with a devil-may-care attitude and we set off on the return trip to the ship.

It seemed only fitting that our tow should give the *Take it Easy* another friendly, glancing bump as we left the harbour. It was our inimitable way of saying farewell. This time there was some response as two women came running out on deck, one shouting "Who's going to pay for it?" I considered it a reasonable question but I didn't have the heart to turn around and reply. Soon we were out of range and we returned to the ship without further incident. Roger, gentleman that he was, said " Don't worry Tony, I will go ashore and take care of any complaints." It had been an eventful day and I was glad when we weighed anchor and Newport disappeared into the sunset astern of us.

We were off Anticosti Island on our return to Montreal when I sighted a fog bank ahead. It was during the middle watch at night and after ringing stand by on the engine room telegraph, and giving a blast on the whistle, I called the master. To my surprise, Roger, the staff Captain, came to the bridge and took over the control of the ship. I heard later that the captain was partying and in no condition to take command. The following morning we arrived off Montreal. Approaching the dock I was on the bridge working the engine room telegraph on the pilot's orders when the telephone rang. It was the chief engineer to tell us that there was a power failure; the steam turbines had ceased to function.

The ship was helpless and drifting with the tide towards a large tanker lying alongside an oil dock. The pilot had called for tugs. Soon after they arrived our power was restored and we docked safely. An engineer had told me earlier that the boilers were giving trouble; the ship was getting old and it was as much as they could do to keep the machinery running.

I was on my way back to the ship after a stroll ashore and met a group of stewards standing near the gangway. "Hey, Second Mate. Did you hear the news? The captain has been fired." " Well I'll be darned!" I said, not wishing to comment on this not so surprising news. On deck I met Serge, the Third Mate. "Yes, it's true." he said " The Port Health Authorities condemned the ship because of unsanitary conditions around the garbage area, and the company have fired the *old man*." "That seems unfair." I said. "Why didn't they fire the chief steward, it's his department." Serge was in a reflective mood, " That's not the way the company sees it. The new captain is already aboard. I think we can expect some changes."

As I walked through a passenger lounge, I spotted our ex-captain sitting at the bar surrounded by some commiserating members of the crew. On entering the officer's quarters, I met a tall, bearded man dressed in white overalls. He held a flashlight in one hand and a checklist of ship's equipment in the other. " I am Captain Teuber. Are you the Second Mate?" he asked, extending his hand. I hadn't expected such a warm introduction from the new master. But I soon found that friendly as he was, he also meant business. I knew that if I needed Captain Teuber he would come to the bridge at once. He evidently trusted me enough to leave me alone on the bridge on the way to New York, when we steamed through the Northumberland Straits, in the middle of my night watch. This was a passage I had never been through before, but all was well and we arrived at the next port on time.

The Captain would often chat with me during my watch; we had something in common. Both of us had served in cargo ships running to the Far East. There were times when I wondered whether I was doing my job properly, although no one had told me otherwise. However, I resigned. The next day the Captain joined me on the bridge.

" I hear that you have resigned. Why ? Don't you like the job?"

" Yes, Captain, the job is good, but I don't think I can cope with it any longer."

" That's not true," he said "You are doing fine."

I regretted my hasty decision after hearing what the Captain had to say, but it was too late to reverse it. A replacement had already been found.

51

Robbed!

The idea of finding another job aboard a yacht had been in the back of my mind for some time but this time I would be more selective about who I worked for. In December 1990, I returned to Antibes and discovered that jobs were at a premium. I roamed around the marina and spoke to skippers I knew and I was advised to try my luck in Palma, Majorca.

Antibes and its surroundings were a pleasant place. I had made friends there and felt in no hurry to leave. I had met the German skipper of the "*Beatriz of Bolivia*," and his wife. They had a car, knew the best places to visit and invited me to accompany them. On one of these expeditions we drove to the beautiful medieval town of St Paul Vance. We parked the car, walked up a winding cobblestone road and through gates into what seemed another world.

My daughter Bernadette, and her husband Scott, drove down from Paris and we spent Christmas together. At the time I was friendly with Bert, the bosun of the yacht *Sirocco*. Bert liked to be known as bosun although he had spent very little time at sea and knew next to nothing about seamanship but he was a skilled varnish man and that's what counted in the yachting world. He had assured me that he had enough "pull" in the yachting fraternity to find a job for me. I don't know why I was so gullible. Bert was a con artist. He had concocted a scheme in which I would be delivering his camper van to the U.K.. He was also anxious to introduce me to his mother who lived in Ireland but was coming to France to see "his" yacht, and she would accompany me on the trip to the U.K. via Portugal. I saw this as an opportunity to travel, but when I mentioned it to Bernie she brought me to my senses. I told Bert that I had changed my mind, he became angry and accused me of letting him down. Our friendship came to an abrupt end.

One afternoon early in the New Year I decided to go to Grasse, having heard it was worth seeing. I was about to board the bus when I realized that my wallet was missing. In a sweat I headed for the police station. I was aware that thieves were active in Antibes, there was ample evidence of it as one walked along the streets beside the Marina. A pile of glass lying beside expensive cars, indicated that thieves didn't bother to gain entry by any other means than heaving a brick through the window. I heard about gangs of criminals who roamed the area in panel wagons, looking for easy pickings.

At the police station I was interviewed by a bearded detective who spoke passable English. We had been talking only a few minutes when a gendarme walked in holding my wallet found on the floor in a record store. Only 300 francs and my credit card were missing, but by the time I had notified my bank in Victoria, and the credit card company in Vancouver, a day had passed. Meanwhile the thief had run up charges of over $3000 in jewelry shops and expensive restaurants. This set-back made me decide to leave for Palma as soon as possible. I had to find a job.

52

En route to Palma

I boarded the train at midnight. Most of the coaches were sleepers. The train was crowded with young people on the move, back packers, students and tourists. After pushing my way through the coach, I found my compartment. There were four bunks, two already occupied by recumbent bodies. My bunk was an upper, and I was anxious to get into it. I was about to climb in when the fourth occupant of our space came in. He was a nervous young American who told me that he had boarded the train five hours ago in Genoa. " Be careful, there are thieves aboard. They are professionals who make a living, stealing on these trains."

" It doesn't surprise me" I said as I checked my pockets." I was robbed in Antibes, believe me, I am going to be very wary from now on."

" Well good luck fella." he said as he climbed onto his bunk. " We won't get much sleep, as we will be at the Spanish border soon."

At 3 a.m. we arrived at the border town of Port Bou. Like most of the other passengers, I got out. After passing through the Customs and Immigration room I crossed the tracks to board the Spanish train. As I walked along the platform I came to where an American girl was sitting beside an open suitcase; she was in tears and almost hysterical. "I've been robbed, all my term papers, years of work." she sobbed. " All gone." A group of young fellow travellers tried to console her. I moved on, anxious to find a seat on the train. Before I boarded, I passed another robbery victim; a young Swiss who cursed the inefficiency of the French police. He had lost his bag, it had been taken from his side while he slept aboard the same train I had been on. I jumped aboard the Spanish train wondering whether I too, was about to be set upon. The coach was in stark contrast to the comfortable French train. It had a drab interior; uncomfortable straight backed wooden seats and little leg room.

I abandoned the idea of getting any sleep. I would have enjoyed looking at the Spanish countryside but the windows were streaked with mud, and so I spent the next three hours reading a book about life aboard a Finnish windjammer. Conditions were grim aboard those ships and I felt a bit better about being on an antiquated train. The rolling stock was probably pre- civil war, and Spain, it seemed, was still recovering from it.

We reached Barcelona at noon. The ferry to Palma was due to sail at midnight, leaving me 12 hours to roam around this ancient port city. I wandered the full length of the Ramblas, (the Grande Boulevarde), and explored the dock area around the great statue of Columbus. I found a restaurant where the food was cheap, and spoke to an Irishman who had run away from some kind of trouble back home. Here nobody bothered him and it was cheaper to get plastered in Spain.

I boarded the ferry an hour before sailing time and was pleased to find that I was the only occupant of a two berth cabin. I fell asleep before my head hit the pillow. On reaching Palma, I found cheap lodgings in a dingy place near the yacht marina, about a mile from the centre of the city. My room was small and on the top floor overlooking a patch of waste land and broken down shacks. It was rudimentary accommodation. A bed with one thin blanket, a wash basin, (cold water only), and a single light bulb on a long flex hung from the ceiling. It was that sort of hotel. I had expected warm weather in Majorca, but it was wet, and cold enough in the evening to require heat. There was none. I wore pyjamas under my out -door clothing, lay on the bed, looked at the ceiling and began to question my decision to go to Spain.

I had paid for room and board; this was a mistake. In the evening of my first day I entered the dining room fully expecting to enjoy a good supper. I was hungry, having been without food since leaving the ferry in the morning. The waiter was curt, saying that I was half an hour late. He pointed to a notice on the wall which informed guests of the times when food was served; even when I gave him what I thought was a reasonable excuse, he was not impressed. He could find the remains of the meagre dinner menu and that was it. I dined on a plate of tepid semolina garnished with a few limp leaves of lettuce. This was topped of with a cup of strong black coffee. After this repast, I slunk out of the hotel in search of something more appetizing. I was lucky in finding a stall which sold fruit and vegetables. I finished supper in my room munching on bananas, apples and a few stalks of celery.

53

Not again!

After a week in Palma I had had enough. There were no jobs on yachts. I decided to return to Canada. Aboard the ferry back to Barcelona, I asked a Purser if she knew of a cheap hotel; I wanted to spend the day in Barcelona before taking the train to Paris. She recommended the Saladin. It was close to the Ramblas and rooms were cheap.

We arrived in Barcelona late at night. It would have been wise to take a taxi to the Saladin, but I was still smarting after being short changed by the taxi driver in Palma; I would walk. It was a longer hike than I expected and through a very rough district. The outward appearance of the Saladin Hotel didn't look very promising, but I felt too weary to look elsewhere. The appearance of the man behind the reception desk did nothing to bolster my confidence in the Saladin either. He was eating when I arrived, and didn't bother to look up from his plate. With several days growth of beard on his face he looked scruffy and when I enquired about the price of a room, he said nothing but pointed to a list of room rates.

I paid the equivalent of $7 for a room overlooking the street. The room was a good deal worse than the one in Palma. After a sleepless night, I left the Saladin in search of a cup of coffee and found one in a MacDonald's on the Ramblas. In no mood to spend any more time in Barcelona, I decided to go to the main railway station and board a train for Paris. The Metro had only recently been completed and the train ran from one side of the city to the other in less than 30 minutes. I got out at Barcelona - Santes and walked along the passageway to the main rail station.

It was a bright sunny morning. Crowds of commuters were on their way to work. I hurried along, a bag in each hand, looking forward to boarding a comfortable French train. I was startled by something hitting my back. I stopped and put my hand on the back of my coat to find it smeared with a slimy, chocolate mix of some sort. Suddenly I was confronted by two men offering me sheets of tissue paper. "What is the matter Senor? You take this. Clean your coat."

I put down one bag and began to wipe away the mess. A second later I glanced up. The men had disappeared and so had my bag. I shouted, "Thief! Stop that bloody thief!" No one took any notice. I wanted to give chase, but it was of no use, they had melted into the crowd of unconcerned pedestrians. I looked around hoping that perhaps someone might help, to no avail. I had lost my Canadian passport, my return ticket to Canada, my Pentax camera and worst of all, my Seaman's Discharge book which recorded every voyage I had made since January 1937.

Recovering my wits I ran into the main station and found the office of the Polizia. " I have been robbed! " I blurted to the man behind the desk.

" Senor, there are thieves everywhere." he said waving his hands in despair. He spoke like a man who had resigned himself to the impossibility of stopping robbers. While I tried to fill out a report form, there was shouting from outside. A tall, blonde Icelander was very agitated. He had fallen asleep on a bench in the station and woke up to see a man making-off with his knapsack. The polizia were right, thieves were everywhere.

I would have been in a bigger predicament had I not been carrying a British passport and a Traveller's cheque in my coat pocket. I had enough money to buy a ticket to Paris but not enough for a berth. During the long trip I had plenty of time to reflect on the waste of time and money I had spent in a fruitless search for work in Europe. Still it could have been worse. I was physically intact, though a little shaken up. I now realized that my search for a job in France and Spain had been a fiasco and it was time to head back to Canada, and find something to do which was safer, and closer to home.

54

The *Medusa*

This yachting adventure began in the spring of 1991. I was told that a man in Miami needed a skipper to bring his yacht to British Columbia. He had bought the *Medusa* from the U.S. Government after the narcotic squad had seized her from drug smugglers operating in the Caribbean. I spoke to the owner on the phone. He seemed satisfied to have me as the skipper and asked if I knew someone who would come as a deckhand. My son Paul was at a loose end, and he and I flew to Miami where the owner Sid, a stocky, cheerless man with short hair and an abrupt manner, met us. The *Medusa* was lying alongside a dock in a covered boathouse at the Merrill Stevens Shipbuilding Yard on the Miami River. She was a 47 ft. Trumpy motor cruiser built of wood, and powered by twin G.M. diesels.

She was a vessel more suitable for inland sailing than an ocean voyage. The interior was air-conditioned and lavish with expensively upholstered couches, monogrammed cushions, and fluffy curtains which made the vessel a home away from home. A thick pile carpet covered the deck abaft the wheelhouse, and a mini bar had been built for the comfort of the crew and half a dozen passengers. Paul and I stepped aboard and met Vera, Sid's wife. She was a frumpish woman in hair curlers and she made it clear to us that we should always wipe our feet before invading her domain. " I do the cooking here, so you better watch your step aboard *Medusa*." We laughed mirthlessly at this veiled threat. It wasn't the sort of introduction I would have hoped for when boarding a vessel for the first time, but having travelled so far, I didn't feel inclined to argue.

Sid had become very impatient with the boatyard bosses. He suspected that they knew he didn't have much money and that he was trying to do repairs on the cheap. He resented the fact that less skilled, low paid workers were sent to work on the *Medusa*, while the best carpenters and mechanics attended to the more luxurious yachts. Their owners were very rich, and didn't care how much they were charged for the work.

My main concern was to prepare the vessel for the long trip of about 5000 miles to Canada via the Panama Canal. Sid wasn't entirely sure about the Medusa's range. It was probably less than 1000 miles. Even with the addition of six 45 gal. drums stowed on deck the range was likely closer to 700 miles. We would have to stop for fuel in either Kingston, Jamaica, or Belize in Central America. Both places were about half way to the canal.

I needed charts, and this brought about the first row with Sid. He begrudged having to pay $12 for a new one. He didn't understand the need for charts for the approaches of ports we would need to enter, or a plan of the port itself. We would have to make at least six stops on the 4000 mile leg from Panama to Vancouver.

To cut costs I went aboard a Brazilian cargo ship in the port of Miami. I knew from experience that the 2nd mate of the *Raposo* would have some old, cancelled charts of the Caribbean, and possibly some for the Pacific side of the canal. He did, and I returned to the Medusa with three charts which saved Sid a few dollars; but he was becoming increasingly testy about the delay in finishing repairs.

Meanwhile my son Paul had fallen out with Vera. She had overheard him tell Jesus, one of the Mexican shipyard workers he had befriended, that he thought the *Medusa* was a boat built around a bar. This annoyed Vera who suggested that Paul was a long haired, no good lay-about who should go elsewhere. To make matters worse, he had told her that there were fleas aboard the *Medusa*. He was right. We had seen one hop across the chart which I had spread over the carpet in the lounge deck, because there was no room in the wheelhouse. She vehemently denied the existence of such vermin even after Paul revealed bite marks on his person. Matters might have deteriorated further but Sid, give him his due, stood up for Paul, having realized that he was very good at fixing things and therefore was a valuable member of the crew.

A fifth crew member arrived. Bob was Sid's friend. He said that he was bored with retirement in New Westminster and was in search of some excitement at sea. Bob had a cabin to himself in the stern of the *Medusa and* Paul and I were given a two berth cabin ahead of the roaring diesels; Sid and Vera occupied, what he called, the master bedroom beneath the wheelhouse. We agreed to work 6 hour watches. Sid and Bob would be on duty from 6 to 12 and Paul and I would stand the 12 to 6. A technician came aboard to fix our self-steering device. It was crucial to have it working properly, as long hours spent at the wheel of a small vessel, rolling about in a seaway, can be an exhausting business.

After two weeks in the boatyard everyone was anxious to get underway, and it was a relief to leave the harbour for sea trials. Now there was a problem with the generator and we had to return to the shipyard to fix it. Sid began to grumble about the mounting costs of repairs. Paul and I had undertaken to do the trip without payment but we did expect to be fed well in return for our exertions. A day before our departure Vera insisted Paul and I accompany her on a shopping trip to the supermarket, and it was there that we realized that there would be some scrimping in the victualling of the *Medusa*.

It was not a very promising sign. Vera instructed us to lookout for bargains and handed us a sheaf of coupons and a shopping list. There were coupons marked 25 cents off a Kraft Dinner, 10 cents off a tin of baked beans, and so on. We were inclined to treat the business as a waste of time and began to joke about it. This infuriated Vera and she began to raise her voice, berating us for our lack of co-operation. I had had enough and told her that as she was the cook she would have to look after the food supplies. It was too hot to argue, so Paul and I went to the nearest tavern for a drink.

After two false starts, when we had to return to the dock for repairs to the self-steering device, and an obstinate generator, we cleared the harbour entrance and headed south

I had decided not to use the Intracoastal Waterway, the channel used by small vessels which affords protection from rough seas. It is a well marked route which extends to the southern tip of Florida, but I did not fancy nightime navigation in unfamiliar waters.

55

Jumping ship

Once we were out into the Straits of Florida our progress was slowed by the Gulf Stream and with a North Easterly wind churning up a following sea; the *Medusa* was thrown about wildly. The steering device broke down, and we had to steer manually. At the end of our watch Paul and I were, hungry and we went below expecting to find supper laid before us by the cook. But Vera had long since retreated to the master bedroom, laid low by mal de mer. As a past sufferer myself I should have felt some sympathy for her, but I didn't. We cooked our own supper of baked beans, and Kraft Dinners.

'Medusa', en route from Key West to Cozumel. The owner's wife was upset when I fell on her precious lamp when we took a heavy roll.

I estimated our speed as about 7 knots, and was about to tell Sid that we were making fairly good progress when I heard the engines slow down. I poked my head in the engine room door and could see that

Sid wasn't happy. His face and half-naked upper torso was covered with sweat and grease, " I am having trouble with the bloody generator. I don't have the spares to fix it. Where is the nearest port?"

"Key West." I said. " We are 30 miles off and the self steering is on the bum too". Sid was in no mood to bother about other defects and said so in a most colourful way. Putting into port for repairs meant a further strain on his finances.

Paul and the 'Medusa' in Key West

We tied up at a floating dock in a marina owned by one of Key West's most expensive hotels. We chose to lie there because it was closest to the town and there were no notices telling us not to. Sid called the technician who had worked on the self - steering device in Miami, and he drove over 100 miles to Key West to make his fourth attempt to fix it.

Our stay in Key West was a most pleasant respite from the tension of life aboard the yacht. While Sid toiled in the engine room, Paul and I spent our time swimming in the hotel pool and wandering around the streets of this colourful fishing resort town. Our apparent idleness infuriated Sid who thought that we should have done something useful aboard his yacht. His temper wasn't improved when I laughed and said that he should have joined us for a swim, while the shore mechanic worked on the generator.

215

The next morning the generator had been fixed and Sid was presented with a bill for $600 and another $100 for dock fees. He was in a foul mood and impatient to leave. We put to sea and I set a course for Cozumel, Mexico. Sid and I had agreed that it would be wise to go to a port where supplies and fuel would be cheaper than in the States. A day later the temperature rose significantly as we approached the coast of Cuba and entered the Caribbean.

We had made good progress and expected to reach Cozumel the next day, but the steering device broke down again on our watch. Rather than face hours at the wheel, I asked Paul to see if he could fix it. He removed the panel covering the mechanism and within minutes had found the cause of the problem. When the helm was turned to a certain degree, due to an extreme course correction, a slack piece of wire had popped -off a small ball and socket joint. Paul fixed it in 5 minutes. Why the repairman had failed to see this remains a mystery.

At 1800hrs Paul and I went off watch. We half expected a meal would be ready but Vera wasn't cooking for anyone, least of all for us. She had something to say about our ingratitude in not sharing Sid's misery and not staying aboard in Key West. Morale was now at a very low ebb. I remained silent but was concerned about the prospect of a very long journey ahead with an unhappy crew.

After another insipid meal of canned food Paul and I were trying to get some sleep before going on watch at midnight. This proved impossible, due to the roar of the diesels and the terrific heat. I wondered why it was so hot in our room and went to the wheelhouse to ask Sid if the air conditioning was working. " No it isn't and what's more I won't turn it on, it takes too much fuel. What are you complaining about? It's the same for all of us. Go to hell."

We approached Cozumel and while I looked for a suitable place to anchor in a crowded harbour, Sid was trying to report our arrival to the Harbourmaster. He bellowed into the microphone but the radio was defective; it didn't have enough power to reach the Harbourmaster's office two miles away. After the anchor had been dropped I decided to seek assistance elsewhere, and while Sid ranted and raged about the inefficiency of Central American States, Paul and I lowered the dingy. We rowed to an American yacht nearby and the owner, on hearing about our problem, invited us aboard, and offered us a drink.

He reported our arrival to the Harbourmaster and gave us sound advice on how we should deal with the Customs and Immigration officials in Cozumel." Make things easy for yourselves. Go ashore and ask for Alberto. Give him $60 and he will fix up all the necessary clearances for you. It's the way of doing business down here. Believe me, it will save you a lot of headaches."

On returning to the Medusa I put the proposal to Sid. He exploded, "I ain't giving any godammed Mexican a dime."

I tried to humour him. "Can't you understand that we will save ourselves a lot of trouble by paying Alberto $60." Sid was in no mood to see reason "No, I don't" he shouted defiantly. "They can go to hell, the crooked bastards."

This was the last straw. Now was the time to make a momentous decision.

That evening Paul and I were in our cabin and expecting another sleepless night. I cleared the air. " Paul, I have had enough, we will leave in the morning." His face lit up, " Gosh Dad, what a relief. I am extremely pleased to hear you say that. I was all for quitting before we left Miami, but didn't want you to feel that I was letting you down."

"Here's the plan," I said in a conspiratorial tone, "Sid wants us to take him ashore in the morning, a heat exchanger needs to be repaired; it will be a one way trip for us."

In the middle of the night we packed our bags, talked in hushed tones, and waited for daylight. It couldn't come quickly enough. Shortly after dawn I heard footsteps on the deck above. Sid was up and about and eager to go ashore. So were we.

I have often wondered how the owners of yachts must feel when they see the skipper desert the ship. Sid, with a mop in hand, stood transfixed on seeing us emerge on deck carrying our bags. "What the hell is going on?" he muttered in evident disbelief. " As you can see, we are leaving." I said. " I've had enough. You can find another skipper" Sid calmed down momentarily; he asked Paul to help him lift the heat exchanger into the dinghy.

A sullen Vera appeared and, in her inimitable way, demanded space in the dingy; she had important shopping to attend to. Squeezed together in an overloaded inflatable we sat in ominous silence as Paul manned the oars and pulled to the wharf. It wasn't until we stood on the dock that Sid suddenly came to life. He tore into me with a

217

torrent of invective. It was a performance which delighted the crowd of Mexican onlookers, who may have thought it was some kind of entertainment put on for their benefit. Sid came towards me clenching his fists, "You have caused me nothing but trouble. And now you are quitting, letting me down." I stood my ground, expecting to be hit. I told him that as an unpaid skipper I felt no obligation to stay. " We are off. Bon voyage."

Paul and I walked way, to the end of the wharf, and into the street. The threats and imprecations became fainter as we mingled with the citizens of Cozumel. It was an attractive town and in ordinary circumstances we would have wished to stay, but I had a strong suspicion that Sid hadn't finished with us yet.

We found a travel agent, booked seats on the next flight for Los Angeles and went to the airport. After a four hour wait our plane arrived, but just as we were about to join the line to board, an accented voice called "Where is Captain Winstanley?" It came from the lounge entrance. I turned to see a young policeman walk in, holding a sheet of paper.

"Here I am. What's the matter?" I said, some nasty possibilities entering my mind.

"Are you captain of the *Medusa*?"

" I was, but now I am leaving."

" No captain. You no go, it is not allowed."

I began to sweat. I had a vision of days, even years languishing in a Mexican jail.

Paul had made a trip to the bathroom and now hurried over to see what the problem was. He was quick to grasp the seriousness of my position.

Turning to the policeman he gambled on the last resort. " Por favor, Senor? Quanto costa?"

The policeman looked nervous and flustered. " No, not possible,Senor."

Paul repeated the offer. "Quanto costa, vingte dollars, Senor."

" Give him $20, Dad."

A thin smile appeared on the policeman's face

I thrust a bill into his hand. With a spring in my step, I walked quickly to the gate. We were the last to board. Once airborne we were clear of the ire of *Medusa* and laughed all the way to L.A.

56

The *Banksland Surveyor*

In July 1991 I flew north to the Queen Charlotte Islands, B.C. to join the *Banksland Surveyor*. On reaching Sandspit, I boarded an ancient Beaver float plane, and, being the only passenger, I sat behind the pilot. I admired his nonchalant manner in coaxing the venerable plane to an altitude high enough to clear the mountains ahead of us. I clung to the seat nervously as the mass of granite appeared dead ahead, then he lifted the nose of the plane and we skimmed the tree tops, and cleared the peak. A band of water and a tiny ship at anchor came in view far below. "There she is" yelled the pilot above the din. " We will be landing in five minutes." We swooped down like an eagle and landed on to the calm water of Cartwright Sound. I stepped into a boat from the "Banksland Surveyor" and was soon in the wheelhouse talking to the skipper whom I was about to relieve. We had less than 15 minutes to talk, and he did most of it. He had not been a contented skipper, having fallen out with the Fishmaster whose job it was to run the fishing operation. They hadn't spoken to each other for weeks. I wanted to ask the skipper about the every day routine aboard, but he was no mood to answer. He grabbed his bag and left. Within ten minutes he was aboard the Beaver heading home.

The *Banksland Surveyor* was a ship of about 700 tons, built in Holland. Before her conversion to a fishing resort vessel she had been owned by the Hudson Bay Company and used for research work in the Arctic. Now she had accommodation for 50 fishing enthusiasts, flown in from as far away as the U.S. and Japan. A large wooden float was secured alongside and a dozen 20ft boats were tied-up there. These high speed boats could reach the fishing grounds in 15 minutes, this area was where the famed chinook salmon could be found. Sometimes sea conditions there were such that fishing became impractical, even dangerous, when there was a heavy surf. The fishmaster was responsible for the safety of the guests when they were fishing. He didn't have much faith in the accuracy of weather reports and wisely, would take a boat out to take a look for himself.

In the passengers' lounge aboard the ship there was a case containing a stuffed chinook of heroic proportions. It weighed in at 80 lbs. and was a source of wonder. Presumably it was there to encourage the faint-hearted angler to excel. The display case had been damaged by exuberant fishermen during a recent party to celebrate a catch. I watched as a replacement was being put in place. When the moment came to place the chinook into the new case, some of the onlookers said that it was not large enough to house the fish. We watched with bated breath to see whether this prediction was right and indeed, when the chinook was placed inside the case it was big enough to fill it. The fishmaster made some barbed comments about anglers, whose sole purpose it was to beat the scale.

'Banksland Surveyor'
At anchor on the west coast of the Queen Charlotte Islands.

The guests would leave at dawn, taking a good supply of grub and some liquid refreshment to sustain them. After a long, gruelling day of fishing they would return to the ship in time for dinner. While the guests tucked into the excellent fare and exchanged fishing stories, the crew were busy weighing, gutting, and packing their catches, which were then put into the refrigerator until the guests left the ship. The engineer, Frank Day, was a man of my own age who proved to be good company. He was a keen fisherman and when not busy with the ships machinery he would take a boat away for a few hours fishing. I went with him one day and thanks to his expertise, I caught an 18 lb. salmon. Frank caught nothing. He and I were the only officers aboard. The seamen were an enthusiastic bunch of young men selected because they could handle small boats. Basil, the chef, had worked in a hotel in Banff and he was an expert in producing the very best food which was served by Lara the stewardess. She was an attractive blonde, who had quit an office job for something more interesting.

I had been aboard about a month when I was informed that the Chief of the local Indian tribe wanted to speak to me about a matter of concern. On my invitation, he arrived with two elders and we sat in the lounge drinking coffee. The meeting was a friendly one; the Chief wanted to know whether we were catching many fish. I replied that some days were poor, while others were good. He then reminded me that we were fishing in Indian waters and if any profits were being made, the tribe were entitled to a share. Anxious not to put my foot in it by saying anything reckless, I merely suggested that he should speak to the owners of the ship. After an exchange of pleasantries, they departed.

My son, Martin came up from Victoria to find out whether the fishing was as good as I said it was. He stayed for a week, and proved to himself that he knew how to fish, by catching a 35 lb. chinook.

A month later I had an accident. The Fishmaster needed to know what the sea conditions were like in the fishing area, but he was too busy to leave the ship. I ordered a seaman to take me there to find out. He ran the boat at full speed in the calm water of Cartwright Sound, and on rounding the headland at the entrance, we were in the open waters of the Pacific Ocean. I was sitting in the bows of the boat, facing the stern and was unaware that close ahead there were rough seas. I would have expected the seaman to slow down before reaching them, he didn't, and we slammed into the first wave while travelling at 20 knots. The bow of the boat was lifted skyward violently, I was thrown into the air, and as the bow fell into the trough I was still air borne, and when it lifted to meet a second wave, I was on the way down.

Thanks to Frank's help. I caught a chinook.

I took a terrific whack on the base of my spine and lay motionless in the bottom of the boat. The seaman picked up the walkie-talkie and reported the accident to the Fishmaster.

On returning to the ship, I was able to walk aboard and up to the bridge where I asked for some medication to ease the pain. I was given a codeine pill and promptly passed out. The concerned Fishmaster assumed that I had had a heart-attack and called Prince Rupert Radio to report a medical emergency. By now I had come to, and was told that a helicopter was on its way to take me to hospital. This seemed to me a lot of needless fuss, when all I had was a very sore back. When the helicopter arrived, a force 6 wind was blowing up the Sound and driving rain reduced visibility to little more than a mile. However the pilot landed skillfully on the platform deck and I was put on a stretcher and lifted aboard. It was a small machine, with room for only the pilot, a medical orderly and the stretcher. Despite my discomfort, I enjoyed my first flight aboard a helicopter. We flew just above the tree tops, following the coastline south to Skidegate Inlet, then we turned east and landed at the hospital in Queen Charlotte City. To my great relief the doctor told me that there was nothing wrong with my heart; I had been knocked out by the codeine pill. He recommended rest, and therapy for damage to my spine. Peter Metcalfe, an old friend, arrived to take my place and enjoy the fishing. I flew home.

57

The *Buccaneer*

This story begins at the time when I learnt, with some disappointment, that I had not been successful in getting a job I had applied for in the West Indies. My impulsive action in accepting a skipper's job on an old ex-yacht therefore, can be understood, even though common sense, and past experience should have told me to steer clear of such work.

The *Buccaneer* was a shabby vessel that had seen better days. She was built in 1918 in Bremerton, Washington for the U.S. Navy. She was 110 ft. long and she had been designed as a sub chaser with triple screws, a narrow beam of only 13 ft. that gave her fine lines and a speed of 19 knots. But she was never used for this role. She was sold shortly after completion and converted into a private yacht.

For the next sixty years the *Buccaneer* sailed on the Pacific Coast for various rich owners, until the cost of upkeep became prohibitive, and she was laid up in Vancouver. The present owner, Mungo Biles, had found her neglected and unwanted and bought her for a song. Now, three years later, he was looking for a contract to provide him with the money to carry on with the restoration of the vessel. Earlier in the year, a friend told me that Biles was looking for a skipper and suggested I go down to the Inner Harbour, Victoria where the vessel was lying, and speak to him. She was being used as accommodation for several young people who, I presumed, paid for the novelty of living afloat. Mungo, a man in his fifties, told me of his plans. I said that that I would give the job some thought.

In June 1991, prospects for a deep-sea job seemed dim and I told Mungo that I would take the job as skipper of the *Buccaneer*. He had contacted me earlier to tell me that he had secured a contract with a company which employed men to do work thinning trees. This would entail our carrying twelve men to a remote area, up Smith Sound, 300 miles north of Vancouver. The *Buccaneer* would provide them with accommodation for about six weeks. Biles must have known that there would be few men willing to take a job with little pay and dubious prospects. He spoke persuasively of the wonderful adventures ahead, sailing up magnificent inlets, fishing expeditions, and all the wondrous excitement of travel afloat.

A date had been set for our arrival at our destination in Smith Sound, but there remained one obstacle to be overcome before we sailed. The vessel had not yet been given a Certificate of Seaworthiness, and only four days remained before our departure. It became a frantic rush and as Mungo did not have a car, I found myself driving from one place to the next in Victoria, collecting charts, lifesaving equipment, and 101 items that would be needed for the trip. A cook had been hired and his immediate task was to estimate and purchase enough food to sustain 15 people for two months. Since most of it could not be delivered, it had to be carried in my old Chevrolet, the springs of which were subjected to far heavier loads than the builder intended. The cook, Peter, a German from Hamburg, spoke English with a thick accent. He would say, " This no good. I am cook. This not my job." It was not mine either, but since Mungo always seemed to be elsewhere when there was work to do, we had to do it ourselves. I had suggested that we needed another crew member but this had been ignored. I pacified Peter by saying that things would improve once we got to sea. He replied that if they did not, he would tell Mungo what he could do with the job.

As the days went by, it seemed obvious that we would not be ready on the set departure date. Mungo was becoming increasingly irritable and demanding. Time was running out and we still hadn't received our Certificate of Seaworthiness. I was putting in long hours, but my efforts never seemed to satisfy him, and I began to have serious doubts about my involvement in the venture. I decided to withdraw and went to his cabin to tell him so. This resulted in a nasty confrontation; he accused me of letting him down. When he observed that the barrage of abuse was not having the effect of making me change my mind, he changed his tone to one of compliments, and encouragement. This was a tactic I was to notice later when he was dealing with the cook. Feeling that perhaps I had been too hasty and unfair, I foolishly changed my mind, deciding to "see it through, come what may." It proved to be a big mistake.

The day before our departure was chaotic. So much remained to be done. But Mungo was ecstatic when the Coast Guard granted clearance after certain modifications had been made to our radio equipment. So far as he was concerned, we were ready to sail. It did not matter that the decks were littered with portable pumps, power saws, outboard motors, fishing gear, shovels, and odd lengths of lumber, all of which had to be stowed away and lashed down. Later that night I was busy plotting courses on the charts. As the table in the wheelhouse was no more than 18 inches wide, I had spread them out on the dining room table in the saloon, below deck. I felt that I was making progress when I heard loud footsteps above. Two young forestry workers had come aboard. They said that they had orders to load two 17 ft. boats on the top deck. I told them that I didn't think there was room for more than one but as they appeared to know what they were doing, I left them and went ashore to collect my belongings.

On my return I found a note telling me that when the 600 lb. boat had been lifted out of the water, the winch had jumped out of gear and the man operating it had suffered a broken finger. He had been taken to the hospital. While I was reading this, Mungo came aboard. He wanted to know the cause of the delay. He expressed no concern for the injured man who, he said, had been careless. I told him that the man was not familiar with the winch and was working in darkness. I felt partly to blame for not remaining on the scene.

After a great deal of exertion, Mungo and I managed to lift the boat aboard. By this time I was exhausted, having worked non-stop since dawn, and I hoped to have a few hours rest before we sailed, but Mungo was in a temper and wanted answers. He insisted that we sail at 0500 hrs. and demanded to know why the cook was not aboard. I told him that he should find out for himself as I had other things to do. I was about to walk away when a taxi arrived with the cook. A heated argument started between him and Mungo. " We are not ready to sail." shouted the cook. "I don't know where the stores are anyway."
Mungo shouted " Who the hell are you to tell me whether we can sail or not?"
They both had a point, although neither was about to give way. "Unless this bickering stops, we are in for a rough trip." I said. "And I

for one, will go ashore and leave you to sort out your differences. We will sail at 5 a.m. as planned."

This ended the matter for the time being, although I had an uneasy feeling that there was more trouble ahead.

58

A bad start

I opened the log book and entered the date, the 6th of July 1991. I had been up all night trying, with little success, to find space to stow the mass of gear that was lying around the decks and in the accommodation. I also had to have the charts and other navigational equipment into some semblance of order. While I was doing this, I heard rumblings from the engine room as Mungo continually started, and stopped the main engines, generator, and pumps, which collectively seemed to be giving him trouble. I could hear him hammering and cursing above the clatter. Again I wondered what I had got myself into.

It was already light when we left the dock and this operation was not achieved without difficulty. A day earlier Mungo wanted to show me how manoeuverable his vessel was. I stood and watched him at the controls as he moved the *Buccaneer* from one dock to another. He took her away from the dock easily enough, but when he moved the lever to put the starboard engine astern, it would not engage. We were close to other vessels in the Inner Harbour and there was a danger of our colliding with one of them. Then Mungo suddenly dashed out on deck, ran aft along the deck to the engine-room door and disappeared below to manually engage the baulky clutch. This done, he dashed back to the wheelhouse to continue manoeuvering.

After watching this astounding performance, I made it plain to Mungo that I would not handle his yacht because of the unreliable controls. This refusal made him angry and he insisted that there was not a problem, and as skipper it was my job to handle the vessel. I replied that in ordinary circumstances it would be, but since he was the owner he should take the responsibility for manoeuvering in and out of port. This was particularly important because of the chance of mechanical failure. I would do the off-shore navigation, since he had no knowledge of the subject. " That's my decision. You can accept or I will quit." I insisted. Later, I had reason to be glad that I had said this, when I discovered that the *Buccaneer* was not insured.

As we approached the Inner Harbour rail and road bridge and requested the operator to open it, the starboard engine failed again. Mungo made a frantic dash into the engine room to engage the clutch. This done, we sailed serenely clear of the bridge as if nothing were amiss. Once we had secured alongside the fuel barge, I told him we would be wise to remain in port until he had fixed the clutch control. This suggestion also raised his blood pressure; he began ranting about the urgency to fulfil the contract, insisting there was no problem with the control; it almost always worked.

We cleared the harbour in fine weather and headed up toward Active Pass. We had not gone far when Mungo suggested that we take a short cut through Samson Narrows. I told him that with the possibility of mechanical failure, I was not taking any such route through a narrow passage. By 2100 hours we had made good progress, and had reached Flora Island. I had not left the wheelhouse once during the 9-hour run, and although weary, I began to feel that we might have a smooth passage after all. As the tide in Seymour Narrows was not suitable for our transit until noon the next day, we dropped the anchor close to Flora Island. I needed a few hours rest. Mungo evidently felt the same way as he emerged from the engine-room covered in oil and sweat, and went to his cabin.

We rested for two hours. It was before dawn when we set off. Mungo told me that he wanted to go ashore at Campbell River to purchase a spark arrester to fit over the funnel. It was then that I discovered why he was so anxious to get this piece of equipment. A tank full of gasoline to fuel the outboard engines was located immediately abaft the funnel. How the Coast Guard inspector missed it in his report was a good question. We anchored in Quathiaski Cove on Quadra Island, where Mungo boarded the ferry which crosses Discovery Passage to Campbell River.

While he was away, Peter, the cook, took the opportunity to air his grievances. He had doubts about the vessel and its owner and had no desire to remain aboard, but he needed the money. He was very dissatisfied with his job, especially the way Mungo expected him to do work he had not agreed to do. During the run from Victoria, Mungo insisted that Peter help him dismantle some machinery; hot dirty

229

work. Mungo could have been more diplomatic in his dealings with Peter but he had a high-handed manner which upset people. He seemed to think he was running a naval vessel and the crew needed discipline. He thought he could browbeat us into submission. I tried to make, Peter feel better by saying things would improve, however, there was every indication there would be further clashes.

When Mungo returned he was carrying the spark arrester, and several bottles of expensive wine and some imported cheeses, all of which he claimed had cost him several hundred dollars. The apparent reason for all this largesse was to improve morale aboard. I asked him why he thought such expense was necessary; we had all the stores we needed. He muttered something about never understanding the ingratitude of men. This sounded like an observation from God Himself.

We raised the anchor and proceeded through Seymour Narrows. With the tide in our favour, we made good progress up the Johnstone Straits. Later that afternoon, a northerly wind picked up and by 1800 hours it was blowing gale force with a rough head sea. We began plunging into this. Occasionally a wave would come over the bow, so I reduced speed to ease the strain on the old vessel. Peter appeared with a grim expression on his face. He said that he'd had enough; the vessel was unsafe and he wanted to go ashore. He'd never been to sea before and the violent motion upset him.

I decided to seek shelter as there was no point in battling the elements. We would wait until dusk for the tide to change and the wind to die down. We turned to the mainland shore and found a safe anchorage in the lee of the land. In ordinary circumstances, it would have been a good opportunity for all aboard to get some much needed rest. Once satisfied that we were not dragging anchor, I walked into the accommodation to be confronted by Peter, raging like a bull, demanding to be put ashore. To placate him, I pointed out that we were near shore but far from any habitation. My attempt to calm him down was fruitless. His anger was directed at Mungo, whom he described as a madman. I couldn't help him so he went to his cabin. I had not been using my cabin as it was situated in the after end, far from the wheelhouse. A blanket spread out on the deck nearby was good enough for me. Mungo had the owner's state room which was near the wheelhouse. He had made it clear from the outset that it was his private domain. If I didn't use the cabin allotted to me, that was my loss.

It was midnight and I felt that matters had calmed down. We could get a few hours rest though I could hear Mungo hammering in the engine room. I was about to settle down for the night when I spotted a dim shadow in the forward lounge. Peering through the gloom, I recognized Peter. I jumped up and walked towards him. He seemed to be holding a gun in a holster. On seeing me , he shouted, "I will blow his focking head off!"

I was flabbergasted and tried to calm him down. I told him firmly to go to his cabin and stay there.

Just then Mungo appeared. He asked me what all the fuss was about. "The cook has a gun!" I exclaimed. Mungo replied in a matter of fact way, " I know, but he has a permit to carry one."

Trying to suppress my anger, I pointed out that, whether or not he had a permit, he should have surrendered the gun to me when he came aboard. Mungo mumbled something about making a fuss about nothing, then left.

I found a dejected Peter in his room, sitting on his bunk holding his head in his hands. I told him to give me the gun for safekeeping. But he looked up at me and politely refused. There was no point in pursuing the matter. The only solution was to put him ashore as soon as possible.

By this time, all thoughts of getting any rest was forgotten. Mungo wanted to leave immediately, fearing we would be late reaching our destination. Although I had said we would only leave at daybreak, when the tide had turned and the sea gone down, he insisted that we should leave immediately. Reluctantly agreeing, I raised the anchor,and we got under way. I then told Mungo to steer a course which would take us out into the Johnstone Straits. While I conned the vessel by radar, I told him to put the engines at slow ahead and the helm to port, to clear the land ahead. As we moved ahead, I soon realised that not only were we not clearing the land, but were closing it rapidly. I shouted at him to stop the engines and put them astern immediately. This done, I brought the vessel back to the anchorage. He demanded to know what had gone wrong. During the heated discussion that ensued, I asked him which way he had put the helm and to my amazement he replied, "Starboard."

This provided me with the opportunity to get something straight. I laced into him saying that I was heartily tired of his continual argument about every decision I made. If he wanted to run the vessel himself, then I would leave, as he evidently did not need me. He was silent, and the matter remained unresolved. The atmosphere aboard was thick as pea soup. Peter was still sulking in his cabin, I felt frustrated and Mungo was in a rage.

At 0500 hours it was light enough to leave. We went out into the Johnstone Straits to find good conditions and the tide in out favour. The meal we had eaten the night before was to be our last for some time as Peter had no intention of doing any more work. Apart from the three hours of rest I had on the first night, I'd been without sleep for 48 hours. The prospect of another long spell in the wheelhouse bothered me, though not as much as the deteriorating conditions aboard.

59

From bad to worse

Mungo and I agreed that we would put into Port Hardy on Vancouver Island where the forestry crew would join us. It was also the most likely place where repairs could be made to the generator, which had given us constant trouble. Since leaving Victoria, Mungo had spent almost the entire trip in the engine room. Beside the generator, there was a difficult pump and an inefficient refrigerator, crammed with meat. I had noticed that throughout the vessel there were various electrical plug outlets, some marked AC, some DC, others unmarked. I'd also noticed that Mungo had a peculiar obsession with vacuum cleaners. Whenever he did appear on the upper deck, his first thought seemed to be the condition of the carpet in his stateroom. Covered with grease and sweat, he would plug in the vacuum, and the whir of its motor could be heard above the din of the machinery. He must have found it soothing, a way to relieve his constant state of anger.

Mungo had asked me several times to notify him every time we covered 40 miles, as he wanted to check the fuel consumption. I tried to explain to him that it was more relevant to check it by the hour rather that by the distance we covered. This simple logic did not register with him. He became more argumentative and I decided to ignore him. The tension increased.

I was more concerned with the navigation, as we ran through the many inlets and passed the lights and beacons with which I had become familiar during previous trips in these waters. Due to the limited space in the cluttered wheelhouse, the chart had to be folded to the size of a book. Constant reference to it with the aid of a flashlight while steering at the same time, increased my fatigue and it was in this condition that I suddenly realised that I had lost track of the vessel's progress. I did not know where we were. The vessel was equipped with an automatic pilot, but I didn't trust it, as it tended to wander off course, probably due to faulty electrical contacts.

We were in no immediate danger. It was almost light but the visibility was no more than 3 miles. I was unable to recognize the land; any mariner who has found himself in this predicament will know how it feels. I do not remember how long this uncertainty lasted but the frantic urgency to fix our position overcame my exhaustion. I did not want to slow the engines for fear of bringing Mungo up on deck, asking where we were. A chain of islands lay about 5 miles east of Port Hardy and, to my intense relief, I sighted them and knew where we were.

By 1100 hours, Mungo and I had agreed that we had made up some lost time and could look for a place to anchor. He wanted to work on the machinery before going into port. I, on the other hand, was anxious to put Peter ashore as soon as possible. I decided to carry on into port. Dizzy with fatigue, I made a mistake as we entered the harbour. I took the vessel on the wrong side of a marker beacon because I did not look carefully enough at the chart. Fortunately, there was enough water under our keel to enable us to pass clear. I was so tired I was almost past caring. We anchored amidst several fishing vessels in the nick of time, as our main generator packed up completely. This meant we had no radar or other equipment that we might have had to depend on. Mungo repeated the refrain I'd heard a dozen times before. "I cannot understand it; it was working perfectly before." This applied to everything that broke down. I remarked that his yacht was proving to be a real can of worms; from the look on his face, for a moment I thought he was going to hit me.

We made radio contact with the shore and heard that twelve forestry workers were waiting to come aboard. I looked forward to their company, not relishing the thought of being left alone with Mungo now that Peter was getting ready to leave. Mungo and he were having their final heated argument. All through the exchange of insults, Peter was demanding the $660 he was owed. Mungo suddenly changed his tone when he understood he was about to lose the cook. "Peter, you are a great cook! You can do it." An odd statement in view of the fact that Peter had produced only one meal in two days. "We can have a great time. come on, give it a go." Seeing that Peter was determined to leave, Mungo reverted to insult. "You idiot! You're letting me down! Here's your money, get off my boat." Before Peter left, he came to say goodbye. He told me Mungo had given him a cheque for only $400. I

234

shook his hand and wished him luck. He then climbed into the boat and was gone. Angry at Peter's desertion, Mungo became even angrier when I told him he had handled the situation badly.

60

The final straw

The forestry workers arrived. They were young people, mostly university students on their summer jobs. With few exceptions, they were a bright and cheerful crowd who seemed delighted to be "aboard a fun boat with promise of high adventure." One student was a girl, which meant finding a single cabin aboard a crowded vessel. Since mine was the only single-berthed cabin, I gave it to her. It mattered little as I never used it anyway. I stowed my belongings elsewhere. As there were insufficient berths, Mungo found some cots and mattresses which we laid out wherever space allowed. I took the opportunity to muster everyone to give them instructions about what to do in an emergency. They listened attentively and for awhile it seemed that we might have the makings of a happy ship's company.

It was late, and I began to think about sailing, as we had to reach our destination in Smith's Sound at 1400 hours the following day. We had to cross the open waters of Queen Charlotte Sound, with the possibility of rough weather. I made a check around the decks to make sure that all loose gear, and there was a lot of it, was lashed down properly. I spoke to some fisherman nearby who advised me to cross the Sound after midnight, when the wind was normally light. Since our arrival in Port Hardy, two technicians had been at work on the generator. Mungo had gone ashore in search of a new cook so I went down to the engine room to see what progress they were making. The technicians laughed when I spoke to them. They said they had never seen such antiquated equipment and were surprised that the electrical supply worked at all. Any repairs that they made would be improvised as no spare parts were available. I got the impression the repairs would be temporary and more breakdowns could be expected. They worked for several hours on the generator and eventually got it going. Mungo was presented with a hefty bill for the work.

At 2100 hours we raised the anchor and put to sea. Our passengers were tired after a long day of travel and had gone to their beds. Fortunately none of them had asked for food. Mungo and I had not had a meal for 24 hours; I suppose that both of us needed rest more than food. As we headed north towards the Sound, we met two large cruise ships travelling south, they swept past impressively, a blaze of lights reflecting in the calm sea. We rolled in their wakes. Once in the Queen Charlotte Sound, with thousands of miles of open water to the west, a low swell made us roll but not enough to be unpleasant.

At daybreak we were off Egg Island; we turned east and entered Smith Sound. Shortly after this, the radar ceased to function. I knew immediately the generator had packed up once again. This meant that fixing our position would now be entirely a matter of guesswork–visual recognition of points of land, and estimates of our distance from them. Compass bearings were not possible since there was no azimuth ring, and the compass sat so low observations of the land could not be made. But the weather was clear and I had a good chart, so there was no reason to be unduly worried. Smith Sound is one of many similar bodies of water in the region, a wide deep channel running to the mainland of British Columbia. It is about 15 miles long and at the point where it becomes divided, it is called Smith Inlet. Trevor, the foreman of the forestry crew, had been working in the Inlet for several summers and knew the area where we had to go. He produced a survey map and indicated a spot called Wyclees Lagoon, where the crew would be working. I had been to the Canadian Hydrographic Chart Department in Victoria to obtain information on Smith Sound, and learned that although a survey of the area had been done in the upper part of Smith Inlet, no chart was available.

The map which Trevor, the foreman in charge of the forestry workers, had, was a blurred reprint. No water depths were shown and it was useless for navigation purposes, it merely showed an indistinct gap on the shoreline through which we were expected to take the vessel. Trevor assured us that other vessels as large as ours had been in there, though he admitted he did not know how deep the inlet was.

At this point it is necessary to explain to the reader that the customary role of the Master did not apply in this case. I had told Mungo before we left Victoria I would not be responsible for handling the vessel for reasons already stated. I would act as navigator in open waters only. It was his vessel and up to a point, he could do with it what he liked; however, the responsibility for the safety of the passengers was mine, hence an arbitrary line of jurisdiction had to be drawn. Herein lies the problem of taking jobs aboard private yachts. With constant interference by the owner the Master's position becomes compromised.

By noon we had reached the Narrows and I handed over the controls to Mungo. The starboard engine reversing control was still giving trouble, which meant that Mungo had to, once again, perform the antics already described. We entered the channel which I estimated at no more than 150 feet wide and there did not appear to be enough water. I advised Mungo to go no farther; he should back out of the channel into deep water.

Fortunately the machinery functioned and we stopped and lay-off the entrance to wait for the tide to rise, which according to the tide book would be in 2 hours. I told Mungo that I was going below to rest and to call me before we entered the channel. I found a quiet spot to lie down and had been in deep sleep for less than an hour when I woke up, startled by the sound of the engines running. By the time I reached the wheelhouse, Mungo had taken the vessel into the channel and he asked me to watch the echo-sounder. There appeared to be enough water as we entered beautiful Wyclees Lagoon and anchored in 4 fathoms.

The work crew was anxious to get ashore to find a suitable base for their equipment, and while they did this Mungo and I went off in the inflatable to look for a more suitable anchorage. After about an hour we were unable to find one, and decided it would be better to look outside the Lagoon where we would be less influenced by the tide. There was a possibility that we could lie close to the shore in deep water and secure the vessel to tree stumps. I returned aboard to look at the tide book and I noticed that the vessel had taken a 3 degree list to starboard which soon increased to 6 degrees. We were aground.

I ordered everyone off into the workboat and went with them to check the vessel fore and aft. She was not making any water and there was no apparent damage as she was lying on a mudbank. During the next hour the list increased to 20 degrees and as she fell over, everything that was not secured fell to the deck. I heard drawers of cabinets slide open and their contents fall out; the galley was a shambles as pots, pans, plates, cutlery, boxes of fruit, tins of flour and tins of grease landed on the deck. Mungo's stateroom looked as though it had been hit by a tornado where books, potted plants, earth from the pots and mementos of his past exploits littered the carpet.

Mungo returned aboard and we discussed the latest development. To my surprise, he did not appear particularly upset. We agreed that we had to move the vessel at the next high water which was shortly after midnight. By 1700 hours, the vessel had righted herself with the incoming tide and the forestry crew came back aboard. After a day in the bush they were tired and hungry. In good spirits they joked about, " the old tub looking like a beached whale". I did not feel in any mood to laugh and was apprehensive about what the night would bring.

I was out on deck and watched a float plane land on the water near us. It had brought our new cook recruited at short notice in Port Hardy. The door opened and a 25-year old girl stepped out onto the float to wait to be brought aboard. She carried two large cases and a parrot in a cage. I helped her aboard and showed her the galley. If she was taken aback by the mess, she did not show it, possibly she had seen galleys in worse condition than ours. I spent some time showing her where the food was, although some of it was scattered about the deck and I asked whether she could cook something up for dinner.

She rose to the occasion and within two hours produced a good meal which was served in the dining room, despite the owner's restriction. Earlier Mungo had expressly put the room off-limits as he did not want it used. The crew was happy to be back aboard, and after a good meal all they wanted was rest. Undeterred by the recent events the grounding episode was discussed light-heartedly, as an experience to tell the folks back home.

After we had eaten our meal I noticed that Mungo was nowhere to be seen. Feeling some concern, I went down to the engine room with a flashlight to look for him in the pitch dark. There was no sign of him anywhere. I wondered if he might have gone off in the inflatable. I decided to have a look in his stateroom. I found him lying down, his face covered in grime, in a state of complete exhaustion. I shook him back to consciousness and made him a cup of strong coffee. I told him he was of no use to himself or the vessel by driving himself into this state through lack of food and sleep. He said nothing until the cook arrived with a large plate of food. A discussion followed about the decision to move the vessel.

With a meal inside him, he returned to his normal aggressive self. He was gung-ho to move after midnight despite the fact that it we had no radar to guide us in the pitch dark. We were in a dilemma. If we did not move the vessel, she would fall over at the next low tide. On the other hand, leaving in total darkness was a risky operation that could endanger all of us. He cast these fears aside; he had faith in himself and his vessel and if I wouldn't take the vessel out, he would.

At midnight it was cold and raining heavily. The idea of sending the passengers ashore was rejected as they were all asleep. In retrospect, I can now say that I would have done things differently, but the urgency of the moment dictated that we must move the vessel at once. High water was at 0100 hours. Mungo and I were alone in the wheelhouse, all was still. A barely visible line of trees surrounded us. I told Mungo that I would operate the searchlight while he controlled the engines and steering. The anchor was lifted and there was the usual performance of the stubborn starboard engine. Mungo alternately cursed and shouted at his uncertain machinery while I swung the light rapidly from side to side in a frantic search for the entrance to the Lagoon.

It was impossible to tell which way we were being swept by the tide. Although it was supposed to be slack water, our rapid movement past the shore indicated that it was running out fast. Under normal conditions a vessel's heading can be determined by looking at the compass. I was unable to read it because Mungo was in the way as he worked the controls, and the compass light was too dim. Mungo was now jumping about and he shouted, " Where the hell are we? Where's the entrance?"

All we could see ahead was the unbroken line of trees silhoutted in the darkness. Suddenly an opening did appear in the beam of light and we shot towards it. Within less time than it takes to read this, the beach was so close on either side that a stone could easily have been tossed ashore. In all my time at sea I've never been in a worse situation. My heart was thumping wildly as I swung the light rapidly from side to side. The vessel took a sheer to starboard. We hurtled through the narrow gap with the awful sound of branches being torn away against our side. Mungo shrieked with anguish but was then silenced by a sickening crash which shook the vessel violently. She reeled at the impact.

'Buccaneer'.
A sickening crash and we were aground.

It was a frightful moment and thoughts of doom flashed through my mind. The scene below can be imagined; rudely awakened from their slumber, the passengers had rushed up on deck. There was a lot of shouting, but no panic. They had been thrown out of their bunks by the impact and must have thought this was their final moment. They were very upset, as they scrambled to pick up their belongings which were scattered about around them. To my relief, no one was injured and for the moment the ship was safe.

She had righted herself and had sufficient momentum to go through the channel into deeper water. Before long we were stopped and lying alongside a beach where the anchor was dropped. At daybreak, we realized that instead of going out through the passage we had entered the day before, we had in fact gone in the wrong direction and into another even smaller lagoon. I made an inspection fore and aft which showed that, whatever damage had been done, we were not making water.

241

The skipper's expression says it all

The job at hand was to make sure that the vessel remained in position. I set about this task by asking for volunteers. There was immediate response from the forestry crew. Two of them scrambled ashore with the strongest mooring line from the bow, and shackled the eye of the line around the stoutest tree they could find. The same thing was done at the stern. The port anchor was loaded into a boat and taken off about 150 feet and dropped over the side to hold our bow firmly in position. I had tried to contact the Coast Guard. At first I had no success, as we had been temporarily knocked off the air. I finally managed to get through to Alert Bay Radio Station and make a report of our situation. Karen, the cook, had been badly shaken up; she had been aboard only half a day and was now in a shipwreck. She wanted to go ashore immediately, however, first, she had to find her diamond earrings, which were lost when she was thrown from her bunk. The parrot was silent but unperturbed.

Getting about the vessel was difficult for them with forestry equipment and personal belongings scattered all over the place. Mungo seemed to be in a trance and then he announced that everything was all right. No matter what had happened, he would carry on with the contract. Radio contact was made with the forestry boss in Port Hardy. The work crew aboard wanted to know what their work prospects were. Mungo was told of the situation and arrangements were made to send in two planes to remove the passengers.

At this point I had grave misgivings about the prospect of remaining with Mungo aboard the disabled vessel. Further inspection had revealed damage to the rudder which was jammed over at 30 degrees and no doubt the propellers were also worse for wear, having passed over rocks. Mungo jumped overboard with his Scuba outfit. On his return aboard, he said that as far as he could tell, the propellers were all right. He called the forestry crew around him, and I listened in astonishment as he assured them that all was well. The vessel would be used as agreed and he would fulfil the contract. Losing money was more than he could stomach.

He then called the forestry boss in Port Hardy and told him the same thing. Perplexed, the boss asked how Mungo proposed to do this with a disabled vessel. Mungo replied that he would move the vessel to wherever the boss wished. I immediately saw a way out. I took the phone from Mungo and said," The owner has told you that the vessel will be moved. As the skipper, I'm telling you that this vessel is not seaworthy, the rudder is damaged. If he moves her, I will not be responsible and will not be aboard." After this telephone conversation there was a heated exchange between Mungo and me. He accused me of letting him down, and went on to say that no matter what I did, he would move the vessel himself. As for the rudder, " I will fix it myself!" When I enquired how he was going to do that, he replied that he would dive under the ship and "bend it back." This preposterous statement confirmed my suspicion that I was talking to a lunatic.

Mungo went to his stateroom. Perhaps he was considering using the vacuum cleaner. I took the opportunity to scribble pertinent facts into the log book, including an entry to the effect that the owner intended to move the vessel in a damaged condition. Trevor was at hand when Mungo had declared this intention, and he signed the log as a witness. I asked Trevor if he thought there would be room for me on the plane. He replied, "Don't worry, we will find room." At 0600 hours, two float planes arrived. A feeling of great relief swept over me. I could see no reason for staying once the passengers were off. One plane took off with six people and as much gear as could be loaded. I began to wonder if there really would be room for me on the other.

Mungo appeared looking tired and forlorn; he made a last ditch attempt to persuade me to change my mind. I told him that in light of what had happened since we left Victoria, I had no intention of remaining aboard. He then became belligerent, blaming me for all his problems. At this inopportune moment, I broached the subject of money; wages' and expenses owed. I pointed out that I had paid for charts and various galley equipment out of my own pocket. This request put him in an even worse frame of mind. He spoke of ruin and disaster. Any feelings of sympathy I might have had for him in the beginning had long since foundered. "How much does it amount to?" he growled. "$1100," I replied. Mungo wrote me a check for $400.

I went below to collect my belongings and saw Mungo in the passenger accommodation. He was crawling under one of the bunks and using a hammer to break away pieces of wood to gain access to the bilges. He was searching for the cook's lost earrings which presumably had fallen down from her bunk into the bilge. It was time to leave. I stood on the stern ready to jump onto the float. Mungo came up to me, holding two large plastic bags. "Do me a favour?" he said. "What is it?" I asked. "Will you take these bags of garbage with you?" I could think of no reply to such an inane request.

He then turned to the cook who was ready to board the plane, parrot and cage in hand. "Karen, will you take the garbage?" She said forthrightly," The plane is here. I'm going on it and I'm not taking any of your goddamned garbage!" I stepped over the rail and followed Karen into the plane. As we taxied off, I looked back and saw a forlorn Mungo raising his hand in farewell. A day later I reached Victoria, mentally and physically exhausted. I had had enough. My seagoing days were over.

Appendix

Note from my daughter: 'My 71-year old Dad arrived at our home in Victoria, exhausted after hitching all the way down from Port Hardy. I have always been respectful of his great enthusiasm for adventuring, but I was a little concerned that he was getting a bit too much adventure for his own liking, and, his children's comfort. As tactfully as possible, I suggested that perhaps it was time to hang up his astrolab and move on to safer anchorages. I taught him how to use the computer. He learned how to type, cursing in the polite, religious way he does. And full steam ahead, he churned out 2 volumes of memoirs of his 55 years at sea. It is fitting that he finish up volume 3 with the adventure on the doomed *Buccaneer*. And I'm glad he accepted my suggestion. I don't want my 'auld' Dad to end up prematurely in Davy Jones' locker.' Veronica.

Sequel

A week after returning to Victoria, I went to see Peter the erstwhile cook. He gave me a cup of coffee and we talked about the miserable adventure we shared aboard the *Buccaneer*. His cheque had bounced-so had mine, but he was in good spirits having been promised a job as a cook in a logging camp. Sadly, a month later he was killed in a car accident.

The *Buccaneer* was eventually taken to Alert Bay where temporary repairs were made. I heard reports about her lying idle for months in Port Orchard, Washington. In 1999 a shipping magazine printed a picture of her. She had come to grief in Tofino, on the West Coast. It appears that she had been placed in a floating dock which was too small for a vessel of her length, the result was she broke her back. A sorry end for any vessel.

For further details of Volume. I., The First Eleven years at Sea; 1937-1947, and Volume II., The Next Ten Years at Sea; 1948-1957. Or to contact the author directly, please write to:

Tony Winstanley,
406 - 1159 Beach Drive,
Victoria, B.C., Canada
V8S 2N2.
Telephone (250) 592-1928